Explaining
# THE TRINITY
to Muslims

# Explaining
# THE TRINITY
## to Muslims

A Personal Reflection on the Biblical Teaching in Light
of the Theological Criteria of Islam

Carlos Madrigal

**WILLIAM CAREY**
LIBRARY

Published by William Carey Library
1605 E. Elizabeth Street
Pasadena, CA 91104 | www.missionbooks.org

Kelley K. Wolfe, editor
Brad Koenig, copyeditor
James and Joyce Phillips, translators
Rose Lee-Norman, indexer
Amanda Valloza, graphic designer

William Carey Library is a ministry of the
U.S. Center for World Mission
Pasadena, CA | www.uscwm.org

Printed in the United States of America

15 14 13 12 11    8 7 6 5 4 BP1000

Library of Congress Cataloging-in-Publication Data

Madrigal, Carlos.
    Explaining the trinity to Muslims : a personal reflection on the biblical teaching in light of the theological criteria of Islam / by Carlos Madrigal ; English translation by James & Joyce Phillips.
        p. cm.
    Revised edition of: Üçlübirlik ne demek. 1994
    Includes bibliographical references and index.
    ISBN 978-0-87808-525-5
    1. Trinity. 2. Missions to Muslims. 3. Christianity and other religions--Islam. 4. Islam--Relations--Christianity. I. Madrigal, Carlos. Üçlübirlik ne demek. II. Title.
    BT111.3.M29 2009
    231'.044--dc22
                            2010048054

# CONTENTS

# Preface
## to the Spanish and English Versions

*Explaining the Trinity to Muslims* was originally written and published in Turkish in 1994 under the title: *What is the Christian Belief of the Trinity?* The author, Carlos Madrigal, has been living and working in Turkey since 1985 as an evangelical worker. He has established several indigenous churches in Turkey, is the author of several widely read books in Turkish, and the director of studies and professor at the Ephesus Bible School. He is very knowledgeable about the controversial topics between the "religions of the book" (Christianity and Islam) and offers solid biblical and theological bases for explaining the Trinity both to the Muslim and Christian communities.

After witnessing the impact of this subject among discerning readers with a Muslim background (university departments of Islamic theology, etc.), and having seen the interest that the Lord is awakening throughout the English-speaking world towards people groups that are faithful to the Qur'an, the publication of this book, first in Spanish (1998) and now in English, will prove to be a useful tool to those individuals wishing to explore the subject in depth. It will also provide them with fundamental keys for explaining the Trinity to our Muslim brethren who, by the way, are avid to know the truth.

For this reason, much of the religious Islamic terminology has been retained, highlighting it within parentheses alongside our terms. We must bear in mind that Turkish is not a Semitic language like Arabic, but rather Ural-Altaic, closely related to Far Eastern languages such as Korean or Japanese. Regarding religious terminology, however, Arabic continues to be the canonical language par excellence. In the translation to Spanish of this book, Arabic terms were used as they are expressed in Turkish, since the Latin alphabet has been used officially in the Republic of Turkey from prior to the cultural revolution of the 1930s and '40s. However, for this translation into English, we have used one of the commonly accepted transliterations of the Arabic terms into the Latin alphabet. See the glossary at the end of the book.

Additional explanatory footnotes have also been added, when appropriate, to explain the reasoning behind specific examples or ways of approaching the subject.

From our perspective as Christians, to consider this doctrine—one of the pillars of our faith—through the eyes of a culture and religion unfamiliar with and thus antagonistic toward this teaching brings a new and fresh dimension to any believer who wants to reflect on the fundamental truths of the Trinity and our relationship with the triune God.

In addition, this book serves as discussion material to help explain the doctrine to pseudo-Christian sects in the West that deny and refute the Trinity.

It is therefore a recommended resource for anyone wishing to serve the Islamic people, to pray for them from the "rear guard," or to simply explore the subject in greater depth from another point of view.

It is our prayer that the Lord will use this simple tool to communicate the love of Christ with even more strength to all who are deprived of his light.

*The Publishers*
*Barcelona, April 1998; Pasadena, September 2011*

# PREFACE
to the Turkish Version

The book *What is the Christian Belief of the Trinity?* has taken on the difficult task of explaining this highly relevant subject to the Turkish reader. The first edition (1994) sold out quickly. The reviews received from readers, both Christian and Muslim, were very positive and have encouraged us to publish this second edition.

The new edition has been revised and expanded; certain sections have been written with more clarity, and some suggestions made by readers have been incorporated.

Our intention is to explain the faithful teaching of biblical revelation on this subject. It is not an issue of defending Christianity or of criticizing Islam, but rather of bringing into the light a truth that is faithfully registered in the Holy Scriptures.

In general, and unfortunately, when it comes to researching God's truth in cultures that confront the Christian and Islamic faiths, dialogue is taken to the realm of argument in order to defend controversial or sectarian religious interests. And in the battle to see who is right, the main purpose of all theological exposition becomes obscured—that of knowing and honoring God.

The reasons that have led the author to approach this subject are to correct disregard for and misunderstanding of the Trinity. But above all, the purpose of this book is to honor the one and only God and give testimony to the truth. All who are directly or indirectly in favor of truth (*haqiqah:* حقيقة) are also in the service of the one who is true (*haqq:* حقّ). We know it to be true that every lover of truth will give careful study to these pages without prejudice and will, in return, receive new light on the subject. From here we wish to express our sincere gratitude to all of them.

*The Publishers*
*Istanbul, August 1995*

# Introduction

"How can Christians believe that 'God is three'?[1] Why do they say that Jesus is the Son of God and at the same time they make him equal to God?" Every reader living within a Muslim culture has been asked questions like these more than once. Muslims say: "Never! This is the sin of association![2] Jesus, the Holy Spirit, and the Virgin Mary are nothing more than servants of Allah!"

The criticism against "the Trinity" (*tathlith:* تثليث) stems from a mistaken understanding of this doctrine. And it is a holy obligation of every believer (*mumin:* مؤمن) and of every impartial inquirer, to make the effort to understand the subject correctly.

Those who reject the Trinity do so based on two main errors. The first error consists in thinking that the Holy Scriptures (Taurat: توراة; Zabur: زبور; Injil:إنجيل)[3] have been adulterated,[4] and therefore the verses that support the Trinity are considered a forgery. However, such an assumption is completely unfounded. The second error is the claim that this doctrine does not proceed from divine revelation, but that it is the result of capricious and unfounded decisions taken in the councils of the early church—specifically in the Council of Nicaea, AD 325.

On the pretext of defending religious positions, instead of honoring the Word of God, doubt is cast upon its truthfulness without any basis. Such an intention can never be an instrument at the service of truth.[5] Unfortunately, these accusations are nothing more than disrespect towards the one who, even according to the Qur'an, proclaims himself the direct protector of all Holy Scriptures.

---

1 Al-Maeda 5:73 (Qur'an).

2 *Shirk*, in Arabic: To make any creature equal to Allah.

3 In the popular Islamic mind, the Qur'anic term Taurat (from "Torah" or the Law of Moses) is used to designate the Holy Scriptures of the Jews. The Zabur, the least known, is considered to be another sacred book given in revelation to the prophet David and therefore corresponds to the Poetry or Wisdom books of the Bible. The Injil is the Gospel (comprising the entire New Testament). Thus, to designate the Old Testament, Muslims use the term Taurat, and to designate the New Testament (and sometimes even to designate the whole Bible), they use the term Injil.

4 According to a popular belief well extended in Muslim countries, four Gospels were selected from among dozens (and some claim from among hundreds). These four are Matthew, Mark, Luke, and John. According to this belief, all the others were then burned. In this regard, it is believed that the true Gospel given by Allah was among those that were incinerated and that the four Gospels found today in the New Testament are the result of a scam by the religious leaders of that time.

5 Truth: *Haqq or haqiqah*, in Arabic. That is: truth, justice, or God at the same time (see the glossary).

There is also a third argument that is presented against the Trinity—the claim that it is incompatible with any human logic.

Our purpose is to disentangle the flaws in these arguments and, together, examine the reasoning of this doctrine. This study is based on the biblical teaching of the Trinity. Right from the start we must emphasize that this teaching has nothing at all to do with a belief in three gods or with associating God to any creature.

Neither can we move on without emphasizing again that the Bible (Taurat, Zabur, and Injil) has not undergone any change since it was written, a truth that is fully and amply documented.[6]

The truth about God is too solemn and sacred for anyone to deliberately venture to alter it. Moreover, to explain the Divinity is not a faculty of the mind—as privileged as that might be, but rather is the exclusive prerogative of revelation. One cannot believe that the early teachers of Christianity set out to distort the truth and invent a concept such as the Trinity. Just as they did, we also—who are called in Islam *ahlu'l-Kitab* (أهل الكتاب, the people of the Book)—base our research on the firm rock of the Word of God.

The Trinity is not so impossible to understand. Some circles, wanting to refute the doctrine, make it seem almost unintelligible. There are many things in life that we do not know or do not fully understand, and yet we recognize that they are real and necessary. For example, millions of people use computers while being completely ignorant of how they work internally. We can surmise that most people do not have the knowledge or technical training needed to understand how a computer works. But that does not mean they are going to throw their computers out in the trash. Similarly, as much as we try, we cannot fully comprehend the eternal existence of God prior to creation. But we do understand that it is an intrinsic and necessary truth of divinity. We say that Allah is *'azali* (أزلي, preeternal; outdating time),[7] that he existed prior to the entire

---

6 See Daniel Wickwire, *Yahudi, Hıristiyan ve İslâm Kaynaklarına göre Kutsal Kitap'ın Değişmezliği* [The inalterability of the Bible according to Jewish, Christian and Islamic resources], (Istanbul: Lütuf Yayıncılık, 1999).

7 As pointed out in the introduction, the subject of this book (i.e., explaining the Trinity to Muslims) serves to also highlight some of the Muslim religious terminology. We must also bear in mind, however, that although the terms are of Arabic origin, they are transcribed into English and may therefore reflect significant phonetic differences.

universe. Even when we go back to the farthest point of time beyond what our mind can imagine, we are saying that God already existed before that "moment." In reality, everything related to the essence of the divine Being is an enigma for the human mind. We cannot understand God, but the mind does assent, and logic does corroborate, that "preexistence" is implicit in the very being of the infinite God.

The same thing happens with the Trinity. It can be understood very simply and yet, upon examining it, we can take it to unfathomable depths. This book seeks to approach the subject from both perspectives—on the one hand, to show that the Trinity is a fact that flows naturally and can easily be understood; and on the other hand, to glimpse the profundity of its implications and truths.

In Turkey, as in any country of Islamic majority, nearly everyone understands Christian doctrines according to the terms in which the Qur'an interprets them. Such interpretations refute many of the affirmations made in the Injil or the Taurat, and are due to misunderstandings that occurred during the time of Muhammad. The expression "Son of God" (*Ibnu'llah:* أبن الله) is a good example. The Qur'an categorically rejects that God could have a flesh-and-bone son. It rejects that God can procreate.[8] And of course, we Christians also reject that! However, the biblical meaning of "the Son of God" has nothing to do with physical parenthood.

The Qur'an, in contrast, and in spite of using expressions that are very different and that even exclude biblical claims, at the same time emphasizes concepts very similar to those of the Bible. The title *Kalamu'llah*[9] (Word of God, كَلامُ الله) or *kalimatin minhu* (a word from Him, كَلِمَةٍ مِنْهُ; Al 'Imran 3:44), which is assigned to Jesus Christ, is one such concept. In this study we use the concepts "Son of God" and *Kalimat'ullahi* (كَلِمَةُ الله) as having the same meaning. What the Bible expresses with the term "the Son of God" is that the Word—the Logos—proceeds from the very essence of God and is living (John 1:1,14,18). Because he "proceeds"

---

8 In the Qur'an, the expression "the Son of God" is understood in the sense that God had a sexual relationship with Mary and thus engendered a corporeal son. But in Arabic, Jesus is called *Ibnu'llah* (أبن الله, spiritual son of Allah or originally from Allah) instead of *waladu'llah* (ولد الله, blood son of Allah).

9 *Kalamu'llah* or *Kalimat'ullahi*: divine Word.

from God and because he "has life" in himself, this "Logos" is "Son" of God. Thus, "Son of God" has nothing to do with physical parenthood.

Another clarification needs to be made at this point. The quotes from the Qur'an that appear in this book, and the parallel meanings that are drawn between the Qur'an and certain concepts from the Bible, are not given in order to seek the approval of the Qur'an or of Islam. To make such a claim would be a lack of respect towards the impartiality of truth—by distorting the straightforward message of the Qur'an—as well as an absurd attempt to seek external support for the Bible. The reason for establishing parallels between meanings is to clarify certain affirmations in the Bible by using concepts that are accessible to and understood by the Muslim reader. And I resort to this methodology solely from this perspective—in order that truth may be correctly understood. Finally, I wish to stress that throughout the book I use the words "Allah" and "God" interchangeably, without entering into discussion about religious definitions and without any other implication.[10]

The purpose of this study is not to explain God according to our criteria, but to try to understand what he has said about himself and accept him as he is. He has given us the Holy Scriptures so that we might understand him and love him. To honor truth is the greatest worship we can give to the God of revelation!

I appeal to the goodwill and understanding of Muslim readers and inquirers, so that they might consider this book as an impartial study on biblical teaching. I wish to close this introduction asking God to use this material so that we might draw even closer to him and have a greater love for him.

---

10   In some Islamic countries where Arabic is not spoken, two different words are used for God. In Turkey, for example, both "Allah" (Arabic) and "Tanri" (Turkish) are used. More traditional circles, however, reject the use of any name other than "Allah." On the other hand, the more open and progressive sectors defend the use of the original Turkish word, "Tanri."

# 1
## Is It Possible to Know God?

No one can decide a priori what God is like without God illuminating that person.[1] As it is written, "For who has known the mind of the Lord, or who has been his counselor? Or who has given a gift to him that he might be repaid?" (Rom 11:34, 35 ESV). Any prior prejudice to what the revelation says about God is as disrespectful as pretending to teach God who he is!

In matters of faith there is nothing more important than knowing what God is like—who he is and what is the essence of his being. Because the welfare of our faith depends on the way we know God. For this reason, the question that must top the list is "Can we know God?" If the answer is negative, any effort to understand or explain the Trinity, or any other similar subject, will be completely in vain.

However, God *has* revealed himself. He *has* spoken to humankind about his existence, about his holy will, and about his commandments. And he has done all this in language that we can all understand!

---

1 It is necessary to experience salvation in Christ and to have fellowship with God in order to perceive—more than try to understand—the triune nature of God. That's probably the reason why the Scriptures and the earliest Christian writings do not use explicit trinitarian language; they were more focused on the "Jesus is Lord and Savior" confessional stage than on theological definitions. However at this point we will start with the biblical-theological approach, and by the end of the book we will address very briefly the subject of how the first Christians viewed God and the triune relationship among Father, Son, and Holy Spirit. Nowadays Muslims know the resultant definition from the trinitarian discussion, but they need to realize that the Trinity is not a product of the councils but a revealed truth in the Bible.

As it is written in his Word:

> *"Reading ... you will be able to understand" (Eph 3:4).*

> *"For we do not write you anything you cannot read or understand" (2 Cor 1:13).*

Since it is God himself who reveals himself in Scripture, it is logical to think that he expects us to know him and understand him, even if in a limited or elementary way.

> *"Be still, and know that I am God" (Ps 46:10 NKJV).*

> *"But let him who glories glory in this, that he understands and knows Me" (Jer 9:24 NKJV).*

Now then, as we said earlier, before we examine the triune existence of God we must discover an answer to the question of whether or not God can be understood. Both Christian and Muslim theologians have spent a lot of energy attempting to figure out these subjects. Nonetheless, I want to respond to the question with the clarity with which the Holy Scriptures do.

Human beings perceive God's existence and power in creation. Because it is in creation that we can find the "fingerprints" of the Creator. When we observe his works, we realize just how wise, powerful, and supernatural the Architect of the universe is. "For since the creation of the world God's invisible qualities—his eternal power and divine nature—have been clearly seen, being understood from what has been made" (Rom 1:20).

The information that the Scriptures give us on any subject is so that we might understand the subject and put it into practice. "The secret things belong to the LORD our God, but the things revealed belong to us and to our children forever, that we may follow all the words of this law" (Deut 29:29). We can know God in the measure that he has made himself known, no more and no less. Many of his attributes—eternal existence, omnipresence, foreknowledge, etc.—exceed by far humankind's intellectual ability and understanding. But even so, the logical definition of a supreme Being demands that God be like this: infinite and absolute. The same thing happens with the Trinity. For human understanding this is a mystery, but as we will see later on, it is a necessity for the logic and intuition of faith. What is important is that it is God who has brought to light his triune condition. He has not wanted to keep this truth secret. Herein lies the importance of this revelation.

In order to correctly understand God, besides the information that he has given us about himself, it is necessary that God illumine our minds and spirits.

> *"For who among men knows the thoughts of a man except the man's spirit within him? In the same way no one knows the thoughts of God except the Spirit of God. We have not received the spirit of the world but the Spirit who is from God, that we may understand what God has freely given us ... The man without the Spirit does not accept the things that come from the Spirit of God, for they are foolishness to him, and he cannot understand them, because they are spiritually discerned" (1 Cor 2:11–14).*

If we are ignorant of the true identity of Jesus, then we cannot know the only God, because Jesus Christ is the manifestation of God in flesh and the one who has made God known in a definitive way. "Now this is eternal life: that they may know you, the only true God, and Jesus Christ, whom you have sent" (John 17:3). Jesus Christ is the living revelation (*hayy wahiy:* حي وحي). We cannot say that we know God if we do not know him as the triune God, that is, as divine Being, Verb, and Spirit. Because: "No one knows the Father except the Son and those to whom the Son chooses to reveal him" (Matt 11:27).

The conclusion is that if we want to know God, and even more importantly, if we want to worship him, it is essential that we understand the Trinity. Now we can ask: What is God like? We know he is Creator, Almighty, and that he has many other absolute attributes such as these. But the question is: What is the essence of his being?

## The Unity of God

The cornerstone of biblical faith is the unicity of God:

> *"Hear, O Israel: The LORD our God, the LORD is one. Love the LORD your God with all your heart and with all your soul and with all your strength" (Deut 6:4, 5).*

> *"You shall have no other gods before me. You shall not make for yourself an idol in the form of anything in heaven above or on the earth beneath or in the waters below" (Deut 5:7, 8; two of the Ten Commandments).*

Most definitely, any doctrine that distorts this fundamental truth is erroneous. Polytheism, tritheism, or any type of divinity pantheon is seriously condemned in the Bible. Triads of gods were a widely held belief in many pagan religions (in Mesopotamia, Babylon, and Egypt). The Trinity has nothing to do with three gods, nor does the Trinity detract from the unicity of God. On the contrary, it reinforces the concept of his unity, helping us to understand it!

Notwithstanding what some people believe, the Trinity was not defined under the pressure of the Emperor Constantine in order to find a syncretistic formula for the Divinity, and much less was it influenced by Roman idolatry. The truth about the Trinity, in the same way as the truth about the unicity of God, is clearly expressed in the Holy Scriptures.

What is the first definition that God gives of himself? In antiquity, a name described something about the nature of a person. God has also made himself known through his name. And the name that God revealed to Moses is of greater significance than any theological definition.

Moses said to God, "Suppose I go to the Israelites and say to them, 'The God of your fathers has sent me to you,' and they ask me, 'What is his name?' Then what shall I tell them?" God said to Moses, "I am who I am. This is what you are to say to the Israelites: 'I AM has sent me to you'" (Ex 3:13,14).

In this way, the expression "I AM" is God's own name, in Hebrew: *ehyeh asher ehyeh* (אהיה אשר אהיה). This is the first and the most fitting explanation of God's infinite being. The tense of this verb in Hebrew is "present continuous," which can be interpreted as the absence of time—i.e., as eternity. In verse 15 the verb *ehyeh* becomes a noun in the form "YHVH" and has been transliterated into English as "Yahweh" or "Jehovah." This name presupposes three fundamental truths:

1. God has life in himself and is therefore eternal.

2. God is transcendent—he exists independently of creation.

3. God is immutable—there is no variation in his being.

The name "YHVH" makes reference to God's self-sufficient existence, and his nondependence on anything or anyone. Just as Islamic theologians express it, God is *mumkin al-wujud bi adh-dhatihi* (ممكن الوجود بالذاته), the one who has existence in himself). That is, he is the opposite to all that which is created. God himself, revealing himself as "YHVH" during the time of Moses, made manifest the conclusion to which scholars would arrive at much later—that he is transcendent and self-sufficient!

God's unity expresses the coherence and immutability of his unique being. The unity of God is an immovable truth, repeated over and over throughout all the Scriptures (Taurat, Zabur, and Injil). But the essence of his unity is much more meaningful than a mathematical or inert unit. For example, an egg is different from a stone. The stone is a single piece and is lifeless. But an egg has a shell, a yolk, and a white. Its tripartite constitution does not annul its unicity, its unique life.

When we speak of God we have to distinguish between two fundamental groupings of qualities. That is: his substance (his divine nature) and his identity (his divine personality). Although some distinction is made in Islamic theology between the "substance" (*wujud:* وُجُود, existence) and the "identity" of God (*dhat:* ذَات, selfness), usually both terms—*wujud* and *dhat*—are used indiscriminately to refer to his "being."[2] But they do not mean the same thing. His substance comprises his transcendental being and other similar attributes, such as his omnipotence, omniscience, and omnipresence. These attributes correspond to God's aptitudes and define the nature of his being. On the other hand, his identity comprises moral characteristics and personal virtues, such as his holiness, righteousness, love, and mercy. These virtues correspond to God's character and define his personality.

In the same way, we can differentiate the morphological characteristics of a human being from the personal characteristics.

---

2   In Turkish, the transliteration of *dhat* is *zat* and means "person" as well. In the same way, *zati* means "personal" or "related to himself" and *bizzat* means "personally" or "in person." In Arabic, *dhat* means "essence" or "selfness" and *bi-dhat* (بِذَات) means "in person" or "in its essence," but the *dhat*-person's equivalence is not that strong. By the way, the word "person" in Arabic is *shakhs* (شخص, *şahıs* in Turkish). But *shakhs* could be understood as the physical entity of the person, not only as the psychical one, and this may create great confusion in trinitarian language. That's why regarding the distinction made in Islamic theology between the names of God related to his attributes (*al-asma-as-sifat*) and those related to his essence (*al-asma-adh-dhat*); *dhat*, as "selfness" or "identity," will be used in this work to refer to the "personal" aspects of the divine Being, and *wujud* to refer to the aspects of his "substance."

## The Character of God

God defines his essence with these three declarations: "God is love" (1 John 4:8,16), "God is light" (1 John 1:5), and "God is spirit" (John 4:24).

These are not simply attributes of his divinity but are the principles that constitute his moral being. He is not saying merely that he is a God that loves, but that he is Love. Not only is he the source of illumination for the soul, but he is also the absolute origin of all revelation, purity, and moral standards: he is Light. In him there is no darkness. That is why we know with certainty that no harm or evil comes from him. He is also Spirit, that is, a real being but intangible, perceptible only when he acts. He is the force that created the universe, gave it life, and sustains it.

There is still more: a human being possesses not only a body but also a spiritual being. Therefore the human spirit can dialogue with and have a defined relationship with God who is Spirit. This is what we call fellowship, devotion, or worship (*'ibadah:* عِبَادَة). This worship is verified in the human spirit, in a relationship with God based on sincerity. It is a relationship sustained with truth (John 2:23,24). Is it not more important to know these virtues of God than to simply speculate about his numeric unity? That is why his triple essence is above all manifested in his moral character.

*"And they were calling to one another: 'Holy, holy, holy is the LORD Almighty; the whole earth is full of his glory'"* (Isa 6:3).

The moral condition or structure of him who is the expression of unity par excellence is three times holy! The fact that God is the extreme opposite of all evil is much more important than any discussion about his unity and is the source of true hope for every person.

Maybe you are wondering what all these considerations have to do with the subject of the Trinity. The connection points will be established in the next chapter, but I do not want us to lose sight of the fact that the truths relative to God do not exist so that we might analyze them coldly under a microscope. They are, above all, revealed truths to enable us to know him and worship him. If we meditate on these truths, our goal must be to understand him better and take him into account in every area of our lives.

Our relationship with God must be established on his existence as Love, Light, and Spirit, and on his three times holy condition, qualities that constitute his eternal character par excellence. For this same reason, when we approach the subject of divinity, we must do so with humility and not with a spirit of opposition.

The general opinion within Islam is that the attributes of Allah can only be understood a posteriori, as the result of his being made manifest in divine works. No human intelligence can capture the exact nature of the divine attributes or their connection with the person of God. This is because, according to Islam, God has not revealed the nature of his being in the Holy Scriptures. Hence the famous verses from Abu Bakr: "Comprehending the divinity consists in discovering that we will never be able to comprehend it."[3]

This opinion stems from considering the attributes of God as equal to his personal qualities. However, it is possible to know the person of God without ever completely assimilating the infiniteness of his attributes. We will never attain the wisdom of God, but we can know and experience his love. For example, my father is a surgeon. I know my father, I know whether he loves me or not, what his character is like, etc. But this does not mean that I also have to possess all his medical knowledge. In the same way, even though we may not completely understand the being of God, we can know him personally!

In summary, as finite creatures we can never capture the fullness of the being of the infinite God, but we can assimilate the reality and need for his attributes, such as his eternal existence, omnipotence, omniscience, and omnipresence. As regards his character (holiness, righteousness, mercy, love, etc.), we, as beings who also possess personality, cannot only understand God, but we can also draw near to him with the same personal virtues of love, righteousness, etc. This is what our knowledge of God should be like, and consequently what should also define our devotional life.

Generally speaking, all the truths regarding the unity of God that we have highlighted up to this point are accepted by all monotheistic faiths. Even so, an enmity has always existed between these religions, as if opposing points of view were being defended, due to the misunderstandings we have already mentioned. We will therefore, above all, try to clear up these misunderstandings.

---

3  *Devvani-Gelenbevi*, Vol. 1, 176–77 in: *Allah*, ed. Turan Dursan (Istanbul: Kaynak Yayınları, 1993).

# 2
# TOWARDS A CORRECT UNDERSTANDING

In the Arabian Peninsula, where Islam originated, in the seventh century, a number of modalities of the Jewish and Christian faiths were expressed. The merchants from Mecca had contact with the Orthodox Christianity of the Byzantine Empire. The nearby Ethiopian Empire was also Monophysite Christian. They believed that the divine nature of Jesus Christ had completely absorbed his human nature—from the Greek *monos* (μονος, one, alone), and *physis* (φυσις, nature). This gave the impression that they believed in two gods: one—the Father, transcendent; and the other—the Son, a deified man. A large sector within Christendom at that time was simply ignorant of the fundamental doctrines of their own faith. They believed from hearsay, and their understanding of religion, far from the truth, was reduced to memorized schemas.[1] Actually, in addition to perceiving the Father and the Son almost like corporeal gods—which is the impression given by the images and icons in ecclesiastical buildings, the belief in Mary as the "mother of God" brought about a generalized and erroneous opinion in the Arab world that Christians believed in three gods.

This misunderstanding is clearly reflected in the Qur'an: "And behold! Allah will say: "O Jesus the son of Mary! Didst thou say unto men, worship me and my mother as gods in derogation of Allah?" He will say: "Glory to Thee!

---

1 Apart from circles that bordered on a polytheistic concept of God, throughout history there have always been communities that have based their faith on the complete message of the Gospel. These were known in Arabia as "the people of the Book" (*ahlu'l-Kitab:* أهل الكتاب) due to their faithfulness to and trust in the Scriptures. The doctrine of the Trinity was correctly understood within these circles.

Never could I say what I had no right [to say]" (Qur'an, Al-Ma'idah 5:116; cf. An-Nisa 4:171 and Al-Ma'idah 5:73). The Trinity was then envisaged as being a triad formed by the Father, the Son, and Mary. Of course the Holy Scriptures make no reference to such a triad! It is clear that we cannot trust what we may have learned by hearsay. If we want to discover the truth about the Christian faith, we must examine the sources ourselves, without paying attention to anyone else. There is no other way!

Before continuing with our study, one more concept needs to be clarified. The doctrine of the Trinity has nothing to do with beliefs in three gods, with the association of any creature to God, with deifying certain characters from Judeo-Christian history, or with anything else along those lines. The Scriptures never support a polytheistic faith. Not by a long shot! According to biblical revelation:

- We believe in the one and only God.

- He has no resemblance, equivalence, or likeness to any creature.

- He does not procreate, nor was he procreated.[2]

## The Conclusions of Islamic Scholars

When Islam says that God is one, it is affirming that he is a *wihda* (وحدة, that is, an indivisible and homogeneous unit). On the other hand, early Muslim scholars maintained that God had a great many attributes—attributes that sometimes have been considered independent of his essential being. These early theological discussions, though they may seem to have been splitting hairs, were of great importance. For example, one of the issues was: How does God know? With his "being" (*dhat*) or with his "science" (*'ilm:* عِلْم)? (It is somewhat like asking: How do humans know? With their brain or with their mind?) According to the accepted opinion among Sunnis (*ahlu'l-sunnah:* أهل السُّنَّة, the preservers of the *Sunnah*, that is, the traditional legislation), God knows through his "science." According to the Mu'tazilites (*al-mu'tazilah:* المعتزلة), God knows in his "being" or in his "person."

Regarding the subject of divine attributes, the philosophers ended up defending one opinion and the theologians another, very different,

---

2  See *Al Ikhlas* 112. This is actually part of the Muslim declaration of faith that, properly understood, we can subscribe to as Christians.

opinion. Traditions (*al-riwayah:* الرواية; i.e., transmission, narrative) reflected different opinions from those held by the religious scholars. Likewise, the Mu'tazilites, the Hanbalites (*al-hanbaliyya:* الْحَنْبَلِي), the Ash'arites (*al-ash'airah:* الأشاعرة), and the Maturidites (*al-maturidiyy:* الماتريدي) have varying views from each other.[3] No one agrees with anyone, so we can see how it is not an easy matter.

There are seven essential attributes generally assigned to Allah in Islamic theology: *haya* (حياة: life), *ilm* (علم: knowledge), *irada* (إرادة: will), *qudra* (قدرة: power), *sama'at* (سمعت: audition), *basara* (بصارة: sight), and *kalam* (كلام: speech).

Discussion centers on the following questions:

- Are God and his attributes one same essence?

- Are his attributes distinct (*ghayr:* غير) from him? That is, are they of another essence?

- Or is he neither one nor the other?

The Ash'arites insist that these attributes are neither equal to the essence of God nor different from that essence. This borders on absurdity. It is like saying, "It isn't white, nor black, but the complete opposite." The problem originated when the Qur'an—as the word of God—was considered to be as eternal as God, although distinct from him.

Sirajuddin Ali (AD 1173), the author of the renowned book *Emâli*, affirms that: "The attributes of God are not God himself. But neither are they distinct nor independent from his being. Rather, his attributes, as manifestations of his being and works, are eternal (*qadim:* قديم) and imperishable."[4]

These debates show that if we only use logic to try to understand God, the Trinity is not the only thing that we fail to resolve, but even his very attributes will be a mystery to us. That is why, when we explore the Christian faith we need to leave aside all our prejudices and have an open mind. And better yet, subject our opinions to the declarations made by God in his Word.

---

3  According to Mu'tazilites (eighth to tenth centuries), God acts—i.e., knows—by his essence (*Allah alim bi-dhatih*). According to Hanbalites (AD 780–855), God is eternal with his attributes, and he speaks, knows, and creates eternally. According to Ash'arites (AD 936) God acts—i.e., is powerful—through his attributes (*Allah qadir bi-qudratih*). According to Maturidites (AD 944), the connection between his divine essence and attributes cannot be understood.

4  Turan Dursan, *Allah* (Istanbul: Kaynak Yayınları, 1993), 50.

The Qur'an defines itself as the divine Word (*Kalimat'ullahi*). Muslim theologians have not been able to come to an agreement about whether this word of God is without beginning (*qadim:* قديم) as God himself is without beginning, if it has been created (*makhluq:* مخلوق), or if it originates in its proclamation (*hadith:* حديث). Generally, the Sunnis accept the first declaration. But, apart from the Hanbalites, the rest opine that what is timeless in the word of God are not the letters and sounds but its essence or content. This content is called *kalam nafsi* (something like "the breath of the word"). In a certain way this is also valid in the case of man. Prior to expressing our words in the form of sounds and letters, we outline them in our mind. The words of God, apart from sounds or letters, therefore express an eternal essence or content. Muhyiddin al-Arabi says the following: "The Word is the manifestation itself of the divinity, his holy essence."[5]

On this point, Islamic and Christian theologians are of the same opinion. Every divine action corresponds to a specific attribute of God and is, at the same time, a manifestation (*zuhur:* ظهور) of divinity. The difference lies in that according to the majority of Islamic scholars, this manifestation is not a manifestation of his person or of his being. On the other hand, according to the Holy Scriptures, the living Word of God—the Logos—and his Spirit, without being duplications of himself are direct manifestations of his person.[6]

This question, which remains a dilemma for Islamic theology, has been revealed and made clear in the Bible in a way that surpasses all discussion. And it has done so for centuries! The Bible affirms that the Word that shares eternity with God is not the Word sent in the form of a book but that which then took on a human body in the person of Jesus Christ (who is called the *Kalamu'llah* or *Kalimat'ullahi*).

---

5  "Allah'ın sözü ise yüce olanın ta kendisidir" (Fusus al-Hikam [The Seals of Wisdom], vol. 2, 35), in Niyazi Mısri Divanı ve Şerhi, *Sohbet ile Şerheden Pir Seyyid Muhammed Nur*, (İstanbul: Hakikat Bilgisi, 2003), 180–181. (http://www.hakikatbilgisi.com/his/nm/122r.htm, July 19, 2011). See also: "As the divine speech (*kalâm*), the Koran is understood as nonmanifest and indistinct from the Divine Essence, though it becomes manifest in recitation and writing" (*Stanford Encyclopedia of Philosophy*, s.v. "Ibn Arabi").

6  Another example is the expression "God is love," rejected by the most orthodox Islamists because, according to them, God and his attributes (actions or abilities; in this case a feeling) cannot be God himself. On the other hand, the Holy Scriptures affirm that the very essence of God is Love. And in the same manner, the Logos or the Holy Spirit participate of divinity's most intimate essence.

*"In the beginning was the Word (Logos), and the Word was with God, and the Word was God" (John 1:1).*

As can be seen in this verse, the Word is eternal (*qadim:* قديم): "In the beginning was the Word." The Word is "different" from God; that is, they are not a monolith: "the Word was with God." At the same time, however, the Word is none other than God himself: "the Word was God." Furthermore, this Word is self-aware, is an entity or a living "person."

This truth configures the basis of the Trinity. Three centers of consciousness (persons) coexist "within" Divinity; they are not equal among themselves, but at the same time neither are they distinct from God:

1. the Being of God (the Father)
2. the Word of God (the Son)
3. the Spirit of God (the Holy Spirit)

## Three Qualities of Divinity

We can use a number of adjectives to refer to God, even though he is unique. We call him the Creator (*Al-khaliq:* الْخَالِئُ), the Maker (*Al-bari:* الْبَارِئُ), or the Master (*Al-hakim:* الْحَكِيمُ). No one confuses these descriptions with different gods. As we have seen, God defines himself with three essential qualities:

1. "God is love" (1 John 4:8,16).
2. "God is light" (1 John 1:5).
3. "God is spirit" (John 4:24).

In the introduction we say that to call God Love, Light, and Spirit, more than describing simple attributes, these qualities define essential characteristics of his being. This is because they are different from each other (*ghayr*), but they are not separate (*ayri*) from his essence.[7] In the same way, the sun's rays and heat are none other than the sun itself. Of course, any example or comparison is insufficient, in the same way as a shadow is insufficient to express a volume.

---

7   In Turkish both *gayri* (different) and *ayri* (apart) are derived from the Arabic word *ghayr*.

This is how God has revealed himself in the Scriptures:

He approaches men and women with the love of "a father." This love is the "motor" or the "first cause" of everything; of the universe's existence, of its continual existence and of its purpose.

God is also Light. That is, he illumines our path; he reveals himself to us and makes himself known. In a figurative sense he calls his Word "Son," because it comes from his very essence: "The Word became flesh [incarnated in Jesus the Christ] and dwelt among us, and we have seen his glory, glory as of the only Son from the Father" (John 1:14 ESV). The subject of the previous phrase, "the Word" becomes "the Son" in this phrase.[8]

Lastly, his being is not physical or corporeal; it is spirit and holiness in essence. This means that he is not like an immobile idol. He is Spirit (*rûah:* רוּחַ ,רוח; *nephesh:* نفس, נפֶשׁ), in a state of continuous movement.[9] "Holy" (*qôdesh:* קֹדֶשׁ; *al-qudus:* القُدُس) means that he is separated from all evil, that he cannot be measured against anyone or anything; above all, "holy" expresses God's moral perfection.

When we seek God, we must do so with spiritual, holy, and sincere devotion.

We must therefore accept the expressions "Father," "Son," and "Holy Spirit" not as corporal expressions but rather as figurative expressions that he himself has chosen and used in his Word to express his unique essence. That is, in principle they are three names that symbolically describe God. We must above all emphasize that the concept "Son" does not bear any relationship with the birth of Jesus, nor does it imply any corporal relationship with the Divinity.

The terms "Father," "Son," and "Holy Spirit" for Divinity express the essence (being and existence), the word (communication and science), and the spirit (activity and holiness) of God. Observe the fact of creation: God, the eternal Being, creates the world; he creates it through his Word, and his Spirit—his active power—gives it form.

---

8   In biblical terminology, "Son of God" does not refer to a corporal filiation with God; it means "the Word that originates in the bosom of God." This can be seen in verses 1, 14, and 18 of the first chapter of John: the Word is the Son.

9   The root of the word "spirit" in the original texts means "wind" or "breath," and it expresses the idea of something that moves or flows continuously.

*"In the beginning, GOD created the heavens and the earth. The earth was without form and void, and darkness was over the face of the deep. And the SPIRIT of God was hovering over the face of the waters. And God SAID, "Let there be light," and there was light" (Gen 1:1–3 ESV, emphasis added).*

Islam says that God has ninety-nine (or one hundred) names: the most beautiful of names (*Al-Asma-ul-Husna:* الأسماء الحسنى). No one would dare to think that there are therefore ninety-nine gods. Likewise, the names "Father," "Son," or "Holy Spirit" neither indicate different divinities, nor do they compare God with his creatures, nor associate his creatures with him; the names simply describe his essence.

To call God "Father" does not mean that he is going to engender children in a natural way, as if he had a body. Any person with common sense will emphatically reject such a notion!

Verse 73 of Surah Al-Ma'idah says: "They do blaspheme who say: Allah is one of three in a Trinity: for there is no god except one Allah." This affirmation condemns the belief in three gods, which we, as "people of the Book," also consider to be heresy. Such a belief has no relationship whatsoever with the doctrine of the Trinity but rather with tritheism. During the time of Muhammad, the Christian population in Arabia, lacking theological education, may possibly have had an understanding of the Father, the Son, and the Holy Spirit that would have reflected shadows of their former beliefs in triads. But any doctrinal ideology that approaches that of tritheism, even within Christianity, is a heresy completely alien to the message of the Gospel (Injil).

At the beginning of Islam, some Christian theologians of Arabic origin compared the triune condition of God with the attributes of Allah. According to the philosopher from Baghdad, Yahya ibn Adi (d. 974), the three principles of the Divinity represent his goodness, wisdom, and power. According to another opinion, they correspond to his being, word, and life: *wujud, kalam,* and *hayath.* In the ninth century, Ibnu'l-Kindi, referring to the Trinity, said the following to Abdullah ibn Ismail al-Hashimi: "How do you explain to us that God is one? Don't you know that the unity can be 'one' in three different manners? Depending on whether you are referring to gender, class, or number ... Now tell me, to which are you referring?" That is, he tried to express that the unity of God is something more sublime than a simple mathematical unit.

## Anthropomorphic Adjectives of the Divinity

Calling God "Father" is rejected within Islam. They say: "Is this not the same as reducing the Most High to the category of creature?" But when God describes himself, he uses symbolic expressions that we can easily understand. These terms are called "anthropomorphisms." Both in the Bible and in the Qur'an, physical qualifiers, such as face, hands, etc., are used when making reference to God. The affirmation that "there is nothing whatever like unto him" (*laysa kamithlihi shay'on*; Ash-Shurah 42:11) expresses a truth. But we must not confuse this with the symbols that God himself uses so we might understand him.

In the Qur'an we find expressions such as "the hand" of God (Al-Fath 48:10), "his handful"—that which can be contained in the palm of his hand (Az-Zumar 39:67), his "face" (Al-Qasas 28:88; Ar-Rahman 55:26,27), and his "eyes" (Hud 11:37). In Islam, leaving aside the Mujassimah (مجسمة) or Mushabbiha (مشبهة) who affirm that God is "corporal" (has a bodily form), the general opinion regarding these anthropomorphic expressions is that they are symbolic (see F. Râzî, 25/24; Taberi, *tafsir*, 20/82; Sâbûni 2/449). In the Qur'an God is also described as a *nur* (light), comparing him to "a Niche and within it a Lamp" (An-Nur 24:35). According to one group of scholars, this verse does not refer to God himself but to "the light that is in him." Likewise, the Qur'an speaks of God's "throne" ('*arsh*) and adds that this throne "is over the waters," giving the impression that it occupies space or that it moves (Al-Baqarah 2:29; An-Nisa 4:100,158; Al-A'raf 7:54).

The Qur'an even says that man can go to God, assigning to him a place in space (Hud 11:7; As-Saffat 37:99). Furthermore, in the *Hadith Qudsi*,[10] Muhammad puts these words in the mouth of God: "The rich are my ministers, but the poor are my children." Nevertheless no one concludes from this that God has biological children!

---

10   *Hadith Qudsi*, 35: "الأَغْنِياءُ وَكُلَائِي وَ الْفُقَرَاءُ عِيَالِي". Also translated as: "The rich are my agents and the poor are my family," in Husayni Madrasah, *DSM, Akhlaq—Class 10*, (http://www.dartab-ligh.org/madrassa/Class10_AkhlaqPgs1-39.pdf, July 19, 2011), 34. Or: "The rich are My Representatives and the poor are My Dependents," in Hassan Shirazi, الأحاديث القدسية, *Al-Hadith Al-Qudsi, A Word Of Allah*, trans. S. M. Zaki Baqri. Qum: Ansariyan, 2003) vol. 35, 32.

It does not take much effort to understand that expressions such as these are used in a figurative sense. And if we accept the expressions from the Qur'an in this sense, can we not also accept the expressions of "Father" and "Son"? The human terms applied to God are not "photographic" descriptions but rather, they establish comparisons by way of allusion. No one has the right to compare God to any physical object; this would be idolatry. Just as the prophets warn:

> *"To whom, then, will you compare God? What image will you compare him to? As for an idol, a craftsman casts it ... To whom will you compare me? Or who is my equal?' says the Holy One. 'Lift your eyes and look to the heavens: Who created all these? ... Do you not know? Have you not heard? The LORD is the everlasting God, the Creator of the ends of the earth. He will not grow tired or weary, and his understanding no one can fathom" (Isa 40:18–28).*

In contrast, God can use any comparison that he may consider opportune to describe himself. No one can raise any objections to this. And in the Holy Scriptures God refers to himself as "Father," "Son," and "Holy Spirit."

God created everything out of love. He is the origin of everything. Can there be any word better than "Father" to express that everything has been created by his love? Even today he loves the men and women whom he has created; he loves them much more than the best of earthly fathers. That is why he makes himself known as a "Heavenly Father" who has drawn near to us, because he wishes to have a friendship relationship with human beings.

The Word exists in the bosom of God in the form of thought with life, and not in the form of letters and sounds. He is the one who wishes to refer to the eternal Logos[11] with the name of "Son." This Word

---

11 "Logos" is the Greek word translated as "Word" in John 1:1. "Logos" signifies in classical Greek both "reason" and "word." Though in biblical Greek the term is mostly employed in the sense of "word," we cannot properly dissociate the two meanings. Every word implies a thought. It is impossible to imagine a time when God was without thought. Hence, thought must be as eternal as the deity. The translation "thought" is probably the best equivalent for the Greek term, since it denotes, on the one hand, the faculty of reason or the thought inwardly conceived in the mind and, on the other hand, the thought outwardly expressed through the vehicle of language. The two ideas, thought and speech, are indubitably blended in the term "logos," and in every employment of the word, in philosophy and Scripture, both notions of thought and its outward expression are intimately connected (*International Standard Bible Encyclopedia*, s.v. "Logos").

is not another being and much less another god. He is the expression that emanates from God himself and at the same time remains in him (see John 1:18).[12] It is especially when he sends the Word in the form of a living book (as Jesus Christ) that he calls the Word by the name of "Son." And he loves that Word as an "only Son" because he comes from God! This "Son" is the living revelation (*hayy wahiy:* حي وحي) who reveals to us God's very essence. And this "Son" constitutes the only bridge of contact between God and humankind, a bridge that no one else can establish.

But God is not an object or a corporal entity. He is Spirit. Neither is he a concept, he is a living and active Spirit. Neither is he just any spirit, he is "the Holy Spirit." "Holy" means that he is separate from all contamination and that he has no equal, but also in a special way it expresses that he himself is the justice, righteousness, and goodness of God.

God created the world with his word and with his power. But the world is not a piece of God; it is not like energy that transforms into material and vice versa. God is transcendental and supernatural. He is self-sufficient, in need of no one and of nothing. He is conscious of himself, and this is enough for him and satisfies him completely. That does not mean, however, that he does not establish any relationship or communication with creation. God approaches moral and intelligent creatures in this world using his Word. And he keeps the universe running by instilling his power—his Spirit—in it. In the same way, he wants to flood the deepest recesses of the hearts of women and men, communicating to them his holiness and quality of divine life. Not only is God transcendent, but he is, at the same time, immanent (active within creation).

We can therefore arrive at a preliminary conclusion. There are three essential and eternal characteristics (*wasf:* وَصْف) of the Divinity that are accepted by both Islam and Christianity:

1. His transcendent being (*mute'aal:* متعال)

2. His conscious being (*'ilm:* عِلم)

3. His immanent being or his being that is active within the universe (*mundemij:* مندمج)

---

12 Just as the first interpreters expressed it so accurately: "who comes from heaven and who is in heaven" in their explanation of John 3:13.

These characteristics are nothing but reflections of the very structure of the triune God! Of his condition as Being, Word, and Spirit, or "Father," "Son," and "Holy Spirit." The Trinity expresses the very essence of God, who has revealed himself with the terms of Father, Son, and Holy Spirit.

- The Father; the divine essence; the transcendent God; God is Love
- The Son; the divine word; the conscious God; God is Light
- The Holy Spirit; the divine action; the immanent God; God is Spirit

# 3
## ILLUSTRATIONS AND DEFINITIONS

The doctrine of the Trinity is not an invention by some theologians or councils; this teaching is based on the divine authority of the Holy Scriptures.

As we saw in the first chapter, we cannot decide for ourselves what God is like. We must accept him just as he describes himself in the Bible. Consequently, the only reliable and acceptable source for knowing God is his Word. Human arguments cannot annul his authority.

The totality of the Holy Scriptures (Taurat, Zabur, Injil) categorically affirms that God is one and that there is nothing equal or similar to him. He does not have any associates!

*"The Lord our God, the Lord is One" (Deut 6:4).*

At the same time, however, in the Holy Scriptures we find that the same way that God is one and singular in essence, he is also made known with three names that indicate he is triune: Father, Son, and Holy Spirit.

*"The Holy Spirit will come upon you, and the power of the Most High [the Father] will overshadow you. So the holy one to be born will be called the Son of God" (Luke 1:35).*

And I repeat: these names must in no way be interpreted to mean three different gods, nor as adjectives describing gender, nor as terms referring to a corporal relationship. These names indicate that the supernatural God, who greatly surpasses our dimension, consists of Being, Word, and Spirit. It is something like the custom in Turkey of calling older people "uncle," "father," "brother," etc., even though there may be no real familial relationship.

## "Unfolding" into Three Persons

How is it possible that God, being one, exists at the same time in three persons? A simple example can help us understand it: I am one person, but seen from my family bonds I am FATHER—because I have children, SON—of my father—and I exist with my own SPIRIT. In this example, "father," "son," and "spirit" have not been used to indicate three different people; rather they define three different conditions of the same person. They are three qualifiers that define my relationship with others and with myself. Granted, the physical aspects of my relationships as father and son do not occur in the case of God. His condition as Father, Son, or Being is 100 percent spiritual.

God operates as Father, as Son, and as Holy Spirit and makes himself known this way. That is, he constantly exists in three different conditions or states.[1] We can explain it like a being that "unfolds" into three persons—or centers of consciousness—at the same time. They are like the three dimensions of a cube. These three states of existence[2] (Being, Word, and Spirit) constitute the person of God, which is why they reveal themselves using the terms of Father, Son, and Holy Spirit, which express personality.

Let us try to better understand the metaphor of "unfolding" with another illustration. Imagine the essence of God as pure energy (for example, electrical); in which case:

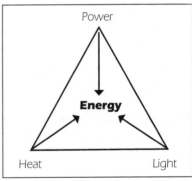

Figure 1

- The Father would be the power originated by the energy.

- The Son would be the light.

- The Holy Spirit would be the heat given off (see Figure 1).

From this example we could establish the following parallelisms:

God is one—like energy, which is one. However, just as energy shares three states (power, light, and heat), three persons "unfold" in God.

---

1   We are not falling into the error of reducing the Trinity to three successive states in which God manifests himself (modalism). We will consider the theological and philosophical implications and definitions of these concepts in later chapters. At this point we are only trying to approach an idea. It is not a matter of describing but of understanding.

2   In Greek: *hypostasis*; in Arabic: *aqnum*. We will consider these concepts in more detail in Chapter 5.

Power, light, and heat are the same energy. They are a same essence, but they are in different states. So it is in the Divinity (of course, this is only an example): the three—Father, Son, and Holy Spirit—are the same God, the three share the same essence, but they are in different states. They are not three different beings; the three are the same and unique being—the same divine substance.

Can we represent pure energy with an image? In the case of electricity, can we see its power with our eyes? No! But we can touch it, and it will give us an electrical shock! God, in his transcendental facet, is also like this. When the Scriptures refer to God as "Father," they are affirming that he is the origin of all things. At the same time, the term "Father" speaks of God in his invisible state of infinite power and inaccessible holiness.

In contrast, light is the visible manifestation of energy and at the same time also enables us to see. God wants us to know him. That is why he illuminates the way that leads to himself. The revelation of his commandments and of his person, are light that comes from himself (*Nuru'llahi:* نُورُ اللّٰه).[3] Light that, at the same time, is he himself. Is the light from the sun not equal in part to the sun itself? "Revelation" (*wahiy:* وَحْي)[4] is the term we give to the action of illuminating. Revelation is the expression in words of the thoughts of God. And in the case of the eternal Word (*Kalam 'azali*), which comes from his very essence, it is one and the same being with God. The living and conscious revelation—the Logos—goes much further beyond mere words. The title of "Son" that is assigned to the Logos means "originating from the heart (bosom) of God." Therefore, the concept "Son of God" has no relationship whatsoever with the physical birth of Jesus.

The heat waves that energy emits are the source of life. The closer we draw, the stronger we feel the heat. God never wants to remain distant from his creatures, like an angry God who destroys you if you get too close; not like electricity, which electrocutes you if you touch it. God wants to strengthen men and women, who have been weakened due to their fallen nature (*nafs:* نفس, breath, soul). The light—the divine Word—shines all around us and illuminates the path. On the other hand, the

---

3   *Nur:* divine light, which is applied to Jesus Christ as *Nuru'llah* (light of Allah).
4   *Wahy:* truth made known by God; verse or word that God has sent.

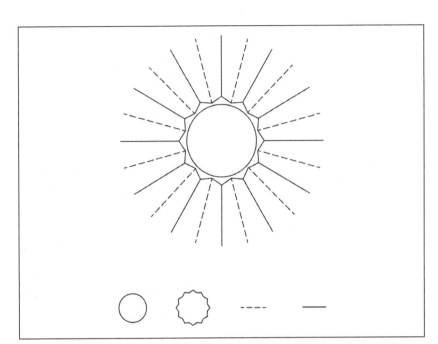

Figure 2

heat or warmth—the Holy Spirit—reaches inside of us, to the deepest recesses of our soul. In the same way, God wants to work in our spirit. The one who connects our spirit with God is the Holy Spirit. When we say, "I have been sunning myself to get a tan," what tans us are the rays of the sun. Are not the sun and its rays in part the same? So also God and his Spirit are the same God.

## The Concept of "Son of God" (*Ibnu'llah*: ابْنُ اللَّهِ)

Our preconceived ideas make it much more difficult to understand the figurative sense of the word "Son." But we are talking about *Ibnu'llah* (ابْنُ اللَّهِ, spiritual son of, originally from God), not about *waladu'llah* (وَلَدُ اللَّهِ, blood son of Allah). And this isn't in the biological sense.

Earlier we said that before the Word of God becomes formed in "sounds and letters" it exists in the form of an idea or outline (*kalam nafsi*) in God's mind. This idea transforms into words, and thus comes forth as the Word of God. But this Word is not something distinct from God, even though it comes from him.

*"In the beginning was the Word, and the Word was with God, and the Word was God" (John 1:1).*

The expression translated in this verse as "the Word was God" (*Kalamu'llah* or *Kalimat'ullahi*) is "Logos" in the original Greek. In Solomon's Proverbs (Zabur), it is mentioned as the "wisdom of God" (*hikmatu'llahi:* حكمة الله).

*"The LORD possessed me at the beginning of His way, before His works of old. I have been established from everlasting, from the beginning, before there was ever an earth. When there were no depths I was brought forth ... Then I was beside Him as a master craftsman [when God created the earth] ... And my delight was with the sons of men" (Prov 8:22–31 NKJV).*

*"For the word (Logos) of God is living and active. Sharper than any double-edged sword, it penetrates even to dividing soul and spirit, joints and marrow; it judges the thoughts and attitudes of the heart. Nothing in all creation is hidden from God's sight [from the sight of the Word-Logos]. Everything is uncovered and laid bare before the eyes of him [the Word-Logos of God] to whom we must give account" (Heb 4:12,13).*

Now we will examine closely the important truths that these verses reveal to us:

1. "The Word already existed in the beginning." This Word was not created a posteriori; it existed from the beginning. The expressions, "before his works of old" and "from everlasting" make that clear.

2. "The Word was with God": the Word of the divine Wisdom "acquires autonomy" within the Divinity, as it can say of itself: "was with God" or "I existed with him."

3. Besides, the Word is a living and conscious Word, on the verge of taking pleasure in something, of making itself known and becoming the Architect of the universe. Indeed, it has life in itself; it also examines the intentions of a person's heart and judges them. Therefore, this Word goes far beyond mere letters or sounds.

4. "The Word was God": this Word that is formed in the divine "mind" and spontaneously "acquires" its own consciousness, is the living expression of God's character and essence. It possesses the fullness of God! It is the "God-Revelation" that makes Allah known to perfection. The Word reveals God and at the same time is God himself!

5. The Word in John 1:1 is the Word of God that came into the world in the person of Jesus Christ, as we see further on in verse 14.

6. At the same time, when referring to the divine Word-Wisdom, the Scriptures use the metaphorical expression "begotten,"[5] since it has come forth from the bosom or heart of God. This is a spiritual—not a physical—generation or begetting. That is why John 1:18 summarizes these truths saying: "No one has seen God at any time. The only begotten Son, who is in the bosom of the Father, He has declared Him" (John 1:18 NKJV).

Thus "the Son" is not a corporal son. He is the "Word" or "Logos" who is in the bosom of the Father, and this is the reason he is called "Son." He is also the living Word that emanates from God's very essence and reaches us.

## The Divine Being, Word, and Action

Once we have grasped this preliminary information, we are able to understand the doctrine of the Trinity a little better. God is personal (*dhati:* ذاتي, in his selfness),[6] that is, he has a personality, which is the same as having his own character (see Figure 3). The character of the Divinity first of all determines his thoughts, then his words, and last of all his actions.

1. Words are formed in the mind. We can say that they are born from thought and are its "result" or its "children."

2. From this perspective, thought, as a "source" that gives birth to words, can be considered their "father." Instead of "thought" and "word," we can use the expressions "father" and "son." The "Father" is the essence of God. The "Son" is the Word that comes from the heart or bosom of God.

3. Accordingly, the Holy Spirit is the action of God.[7]

---

5　The verb "to generate" or "to beget" does not exist in Turkish. The expression from Proverbs is therefore translated in this language as "to be born," which can give the erroneous impression of "procreation." Hence we present "generation" as a metaphor, in order that it not be misunderstood for a childbirth.

6　We must not confuse the "person" with the human being. "Person" refers to a self-aware being having the capacity to feel, think, decide, and operate.

7　Once again we are drawing parallelisms by using examples that are not a "photographic" description but a figurative approach to the reality of the Trinity.

This is similar to a spring of water, where there is a combination of source, fluid, and flow.

Continuing along this line of explanation we can establish a parallelism with the Divinity, with the figurative sense corresponding to:

1.  Its internal thought

2.  The expression of that thought

3.  The combined action of both with:

    •   The "Father"

    •   The "Son"

    •   The "Holy Spirit"

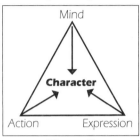

Figure 3

The same thing is applicable to man, who exists with his thoughts, expressions, and actions. His thoughts remain hidden internally; they are the raw material of the mind. However, we—as far as our character and personality—and our thoughts are the same thing. Words, on the other hand, come out of man and are irrecoverable—in the sense that once said they cannot be changed. A person and his or her expressions are in part different things, but in part one and the same. If Murray offends me by something he says, it is because his words, since they are his expressions, in a way are him. They are not something independent and impersonal. In the same way, the actions of people affect the surroundings of the people. The actions belong to the person; they are the person, once again. If Murray hits me, I don't accuse Mike. It is Murray who is to blame. A person's thoughts, expressions, and actions are "that person," they are one with that person. So we come to know what that person is like and how he or she thinks, all through their words and actions. This is especially true of God, who is intangible; we cannot come to know him except through his words and his works.

The Being, the Word, and the Holy Spirit of God are God himself. But we must not reduce the three persons of the Trinity to a mere thought, word, or act. In the example we have used, we must keep in mind that each one—Father, Son, and Holy Spirit, together and separately, are not parts of the Divinity, but rather they possess the fullness of the Divinity. They are each completely God! That is, the Father as "mind," "origin," or "source" is God. The Word, as "expression" of the Divinity, lives and is

God himself; and the Spirit, as the "agent" of the mind and of the divine Word has his own life and is also fully the same God.

The divine Word—the Son, is being "begotten" in the "mind" of God from eternity. That is, he "emanates" from the Father. But this generating act is not in the physical sense. Without a doubt, God does not beget, nor is he begotten. But the Word—*Kalam*, having been generated or begotten in the heart or bosom of God, has been "born" of God. The same way that it is not a physical birth, this generation is not an act of creation either, because it occurs in eternity and in the bosom of the Divinity, not outside of it; that is, beyond the limits of time and space. Where time does not exist there is no "before" nor an "after," so for the same reason we cannot speak of a "first" generation. The divine Word has not been created and is as eternal as God himself.

## The Word Takes on Bodily Form

We cannot confuse the "Son"—the divine Word—with Jesus the man. We must not think that the divine Word that lives in Jesus, and his body, are one and the same, in the same way that we do not confuse the light with the lightbulb.

That is, the "Son" is eternal. His "birth" (generation or begetting) is not corporal but spiritual, it occurs in the heart of the Father. On the other hand, Jesus Christ was born in flesh, on a specific day in history. Prior to being born, the man Jesus did not exist. His birth was physical. But now, the Son and the man cohabit as Jesus. That being the case, what is the relationship or connection between them both?

If my father telephones me, the voice I hear is my father's. His voice is reaching me through the telephone, but I am never going to confuse my father with the telephone. The Word that came into this world as Jesus is God, but we must not confuse the physical body of Jesus with the transcendent God.

God wanted to make himself known to us. And he wanted to do so in an audible, understandable, and visible way. It was for this purpose that the Word put on or took on a body,[8] but a body without sin. Just as inside a

---

8　Here we are not reducing the humanity of Jesus only to his body, but we are establishing the difference between the physical body of Jesus and his divinity. In the following chapters we will approach the subject of the union of the two natures.

lightbulb there must be a vacuum in order for the wire to give light without burning up the filament, so in Jesus Christ, when God put on the clothes of humanity, they had to be the clothes of a holy humanity so that the humanity would not be consumed by God's holiness. The transcendent God did not become "polluted" upon entering into direct contact with the fallen world. Like a chimney sweep wears gloves so as not to get his hands dirty, to enter our sick world God put on a spotless human nature.

Therefore, the Injil—the Gospel—that descended from heaven[9] was not a book but was the very "Son," the divine Word, incarnated or become human in Jesus Christ (see John 1:1,14; 3:31). The most perfect revelation is not the written one but the revelation that came in the form of man and lives as Jesus Christ:

1. Exactly as God put his spoken words (*kalam lafzi:* كلام لَفْظِي, pronounced word) in a book (*Al-Kitabu'l-Mukaddes:* أَلْكِتابُ ٱلْمُقَدَّس, the Holy Book), giving his words the form of letters and sounds (see Figure 4).

2. In the same way he put his living Word (*kalam nafsi:* كلام نفسي, essence of the word) in a human nature (*'Issa al-Masih:* عيسى المسيح, Jesus the Christ), giving it body and personality (see Figure 4).

Just as the Holy Scriptures have divine characteristics, the living Word—Jesus—also has divine qualities. This has nothing to do with associating a

Figure 4

---

9   According to Muslim culture, the Gospel descended from heaven. That is, it was revealed word for word to Jesus, who then wrote it in a book: the Injil.

creature to God; rather it is God who has taken the form of a servant (Phil 2:7). The difference is that the Bible is not God because it is an expression of the Word (*kalam nafsi*), but Jesus Christ is God because he is the very Word.

To use terms that are familiar to us, Jesus is "his Word" (*kalimatin minhu:* كَلِمَةٌ مِنْهُ; Al 'Imran 3:39,44,45; An-Nisa 4:171), who took on a body in Mary's womb by the work of the Holy Spirit. The *Kalamu'llah* or *Kalimat'ullahi*—Word of God—was grafted in Jesus. Who is this living Word of God but Jesus himself? When I hear my father's voice on the telephone, who else can it be but him? We have finally solved this! The Word is called "Son" not in a physical sense but rather because he comes from God. He is called God because he is the same essence as the Most High.

In summary, we can say that the fact that Jesus is the Son of God is not subjected to or dependent on his earthly birth. Before being born as a man, the spiritual being that was "installed" in Jesus—the divine Word—was in fact already the Son, the living revelation of God, the *Kalamu'llah*. He was not forced to be born as a man. Even if Jesus had not come to this world, he would continue to be the Son (that is, the Word), because he already existed in the heart of God. It was after taking on a human nature that he became the Son of Man, the Messiah, and the Savior. Through his birth, Jesus Christ was and is a man; but as the divine Word that lives from eternity, he is and always has been God in person. His body is a human body, but his spirit is the Spirit and the Word of God (the *Ruhu'llah:* روح الله, and the *Kalamu'llah:* كَلاَمُ الله).

When the president appears on television, we see his image on the screen. The television screen is not the president, but when I point to it I can say: "Look, the president!" The body of Jesus is like the television screen. The Word that lives in him is like the president's image. We do not call the body of Jesus "God." But we can call the person—the Word—that is in him "Lord" (*al-Rabb:* الرب).[10]

---

10  In Islam, the term "Rabb," which can be translated as "Lord," is only applicable to God and to no one else.

## The Son: Using the Terminology of Islamic Theologians

Islamic scholars (*'ulama:* عُلَمَا) and theologians, intuiting the mystery of the Word of God, were in agreement that God is the wise (*A'lim:* عَالِم), the powerful (*Qadir:* قَدِير), the sovereign (*Murid:* مُرِيد), and the one who speaks (*Mutakallim:* مُتَكَلِّم). Therefore, among the attributes that are called "*sifat-e-thubutiyyah*" (صِفَات ثُبوتِية, positive attributes), that is, qualities that declare positively who God is, we find the "Word" —*Kalam*. The scholars affirmed that this Word was something more than mere "letters and syllables," that it constituted the essence of the mind of God—*kalam nafsi*—and that it was eternal as God himself is eternal.

The Qur'an emphatically rejects the concept of "Son of God" because it understands the term as a physical relationship, as a *waladu'llah* (وَلَدُ الله, blood son of Allah). Even so, when the Qur'an speaks of Jesus as a *kalam* or word coming from God (Al 'Imran 3:39,44,45; An-Nisa 4:171), although a different meaning may be given, it is expressing nearly the same as the term "Son of God."

Islamic scholars at the beginning of the hijra affirmed that the "word of God" had not been created (*makhluq:* مخلوق) but that it was eternal (*'azali:* أزلي). Jesus is identified in the Qur'an as *kalimatuhu minhu* ("his word," Al 'Imran 3:44), but Islamic thinkers did not attribute personal value to this "word of God." Although according to some scholars the word of God took on the form of a book, they did not even think of it possibly taking on human form.

Consequently, the Qur'an does not support the category of "son" being accorded to the word of God. We are not seeking the approval of the Qur'an or of its scholars in order to support these teachings; rather, we have sought to show some similar concepts in Arabic and Islamic terminology to help us understand the real, but spiritual, meaning of the expression "Son of God" or "Word of God" and its associated links.

God created the world with his living Word: Allah says, "'Be,' and it is." (*kun fayakunu:* كُنْ فَيَكُونُ; see Al-Baqarah 2:117.) The commandment "be" (the divine fiat), is none other than the wisdom and creative power of God, the living manifestation of his will and of his science. It is the selfsame God! But, how is this possible? It is evident from the fact that God does not create nor use only his will (simply willing it in his "inner being"), but he uses his Word. Some Islamists will differ, saying that the Word of God is a substance separate and different from him and is therefore not equal or coexistent with him. But in the creative action, God did not use any instrument outside of his being or substance. He did not create with any outside help because he created from nothing! Where there is nothing, apart from the Creator, God was not going to use "something" outside of himself. The commandment "be" was not the created object but the Creator. Nor was it a "part" of God, because he is indivisible.

At his command, the material created at that instant entered into movement due to the effect of a powerful force, like that of a "wind," which gave it form. The Creator, the Word, and his Power in action, are nothing else than the three principles that form the unique God:

> *"In the beginning God created the heavens and the earth. Now the earth was formless and empty, darkness was over the surface of the deep, and the Spirit of God was hovering over the waters [gave them form]. And God said, "Let there be light," and there was light" (Gen 1:1–3).*

> *"In the beginning was the Word [Kalam], and the Word was with God ... Through him all things were made; without him nothing was made that has been made ... The Word became flesh and made his dwelling among us" (John 1:1–3,14).*

It is said of Jesus that he is "his Word"; that is, that the Word, indistinctly from the divine essence, came to the earth and made its dwelling in Jesus. According to a Turkish translation of the Qur'an, Jesus "is the incarnated word of God"—Jesus is "his Word" (Al 'Imran 3:39).[11] The fiat Word of God (*kun*: کُنْ, An-Nisa 4:171) became incarnated in Jesus when he was conceived in Mary's womb. We are not saying that Jesus was created by the fiat as in the case of Adam (as Islam maintains),[12] but that the fiat is

---

11  *"Isâ, Allah'tan gelip vücud bulan kelimedir." The Qur'an*, Turkish trans. Meâl (Ankara: Ministry of Religious Affairs, 1985).

12  By way of contrast: *"Isâ ... kün kelimesiyle Meryem'e ilkâ olunmus mahlûktur"* ("Jesus ... is a creature delivered to Mary by the fiat commandment of God"); note on An-Nisa 4:171 in *The Qur'an*, Turkish translation (Istanbul: Huzur Publishing House, 1992). The Qur'an does not say that the fiat is equivalent to the essence of God, or that it inhabited Jesus. In these verses (according to most interpreters), it records that Jesus was brought into existence by God's direct command, in a similar fashion as that of Adam. With these quotations from the Qur'an we have only sought to point out the similarity of some of its concepts with those of the Bible, even though some meanings are opposite.

the essence that was incarnated. Adam is the result of the fiat, while Jesus is the very fiat! It is the "be" of God (his Word) that shares his same essence. Therefore, the *Kalam* that indwells Jesus is the very nature of God!

## The Definition of the Trinity

Let us now try to give a definition of the Trinity:

God is one. His essential being (*wujud*), is one and the same indivisible being, forever and ever. This unicity of God is called *tauhid* (unity).

His identity (*dhat*, selfness), however, is manifest on three "poles," such as conscious Being, Word, and Action. This diversity within the divine unity is called *tathlith* (triad).

Consequently, we can define the Trinity as "three" in the "unity" (*tathlith fi'l-tauhid:* تثليث في التوحيد).[13]

That is, *only one* God who exists in *three states*. One sole substance in which three persons coexist—in philosophical terms three "centers of consciousness," or in Arabic, three *'aqnum* (أقنوم).

These three persons are defined in the Holy Scriptures as Father, Son, and Holy Spirit, terms that have spiritual significance, not physical. The Trinity is the essence of the one and only God who has revealed himself as Father, Son, and Holy Spirit.

---

13 The Trinity is erroneously designated using only the term *tathlith*, that is, "triad," by Islamic theological circles. Therefore the correct equivalent to its definition would be the one given here: tathlith in tauhid.

# 4
## TRINITARIAN DECLARATIONS IN THE BIBLE

Everything discussed in the previous chapters is clearly supported by declarations in the Bible, the undisputable source for the doctrine of the Trinity. In this chapter we are going to explore the most important texts related to the subject.

The Holy Scriptures reveal a living God to us. In its pages we do not find a definition of the "Trinity" in a laboratory style of analysis. We do not even find the word "trinity." However, this truth permeates all the verses that make reference to God.

In order to doctrinally define a biblical truth all passages relating to the subject must be examined. The meaning of some verses is obvious, others are susceptible to various interpretations—those passages that can be read as having more than one meaning. A doctrine is determined by the biblical texts providing unequivocal interpretation. But all the passages must be able to fit into the resulting doctrinal definition. It is something like a jigsaw puzzle, where each piece must find its corresponding place. The meaning of verses that are less clear must be subjected to Scriptural declarations that are clear. In the end, however, the doctrinal definition must present an explanation that harmonizes with all passages relating to the theme. In this way we say that the Bible interprets itself.

Let's take the following declaration as an example: "The LORD is greater than all gods" (Ex 18:11 ESV). If we examine this expression in isolation from the rest of Scripture, it gives the impression that there is more than one god and that the Lord God is the strongest of them all. But the gods mentioned here, are they truly gods? Does it not refer to those gods that are the product of man's imagination? Or is it referring to what are considered by some people to be gods, that is, idols? What is the correct answer? If we take into account only this verse, the answer will remain unanswered or open to free interpretation. Thanks to God, however, he has not left us in a quandary.

There are statements regarding this subject that are clear beyond all doubt, and they must determine our understanding. The meaning of this statement from Exodus is expanded in another book also written by Moses: "the LORD is God in heaven above and on the earth beneath; there is no other" (Deut 4:39 ESV). Other statements are made elsewhere in the Bible that are equally conclusive. "I am God, and there is no other; I am God, and there is none like me" (Isa 46:9 ESV; cf. 43:10). Therefore, the meaning of Exodus 18:11 is that God is greater than those that in Egypt were considered to be gods.[1]

To focus on the subject at hand, the main statements that the Scriptures make with regards to the Trinity can be summed up in seven. This classification is based on texts that are very clear in their meaning. It also sheds light on the remaining related texts that may be less clear, providing a harmonious and coherent explanation of this revealed truth.

1. God is one in essence.

2. God is manifest in a plurality.

3. God is the "Heavenly Father."

4. The "Son" is God himself.

5. The "Holy Spirit" is God himself.

6. The "three" equally share all of the divine attributes.

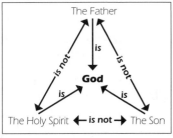

Figure 5

7. There is no confusion between the three persons (see Figure 5).

Conclusion: God is one in essence, but triple in personhood; that is, he is a trinity (a tri-unity).

---

1   Or quite simply it is an expression by Jethro, and we do not know to what degree he may have been a believer or known God's revealed truth.

## Unicity of God

Here are some Bible verses that emphasize the unicity of God:

*"The LORD our God, the LORD is one" (Deut 6:4 ESV).*

*"Before me no god was formed, nor shall there be any after me ... I am the first and I am the last; besides me there is no god ... I am the LORD, and there is no other, besides me there is no God" (Isa 43:10; 44:6; 45:5 ESV).*

*"The Lord our God, the Lord is one" (Mark 12:29).*

*"... since God is one" (Rom 3:30).*

*"For there is one God" (1 Tim 2:5).*

*"You believe that God is one; you do well" (Jas 2:19).*

## Plurality within the Divinity

Some verses express a plurality of "persons"—personal identities—in the Divinity:

*"In the beginning, God created ... And the Spirit of God was hovering over the face of the waters ... Let there be ... and there was" (Gen 1:1–3 ESV; cf. Ps 33:6).*

*"Then God said, 'Let us make man in our image, after our likeness'" (Gen 1:26 ESV).*

*"I saw the Lord sitting upon a throne, high and lifted up ... Above him stood the seraphim ... And one called to another and said: 'Holy, holy, holy is the LORD of hosts; [cf. Revelation 4:8, where the same thing is said of the Lamb, that is, of Jesus] the whole earth is full of his glory!'... And I heard the voice of the Lord saying ... 'Keep on hearing, but do not understand'" (Isa 6:1–10 ESV; cf. John 12:40,41 where the glory seen in this vision is attributed to Jesus, and cf. Acts 28:25–27 where it says that the Lord that speaks in the passage from Isaiah is the Holy Spirit).*

*"And now the Lord GOD has sent me, and his Spirit ... The Spirit of the Lord GOD is upon me" (Isa 48:16; 61:1 ESV).*

*"I will recount the steadfast love of the LORD ... And he became their Savior. In all their affliction he was afflicted, and the angel (i.e., "the sent one") of his presence saved them ... But they rebelled and grieved his Holy Spirit" (Isa 63:7–10 ESV).*

*"Baptizing them in the name of the Father and of the Son and of the Holy Spirit" (Matt 28:19).*

*"The Holy Spirit will come upon you, and the power of the Most High will overshadow you; therefore the child to be born will be called holy—the Son of God" (Luke 1:35 ESV).*

*"And as he [Jesus] was praying, heaven was opened and the Holy Spirit descended on him ... And a voice came from heaven: 'You are my Son, whom I love'" (Luke 3:21,22).*

*"But the one who denies me before men will be denied before the angels of God ... the one who blasphemes against the Holy Spirit will not be forgiven" (Luke 12:9,10 ESV).*

*"He will give you ... the Spirit of truth ... he dwells with you [like Jesus] and will be in you ... I will come to you ... In that day you will know that I am in my Father, and you in me, and I in you ... and we [Father and Son] will come to him and make our home with him" (John 14:16–24 ESV).*

It can be seen clearly here that the Helper promised to indwell the believer, in spite of preferentially being the Holy Spirit is at the same time Father and Son.

*"Why has Satan filled your heart to lie to the Holy Spirit ... You have not lied to men but to God ... How is it that you have agreed together to test the Spirit of the Lord?" (Acts 5:3,4,9 ESV).*

*"You, however, are not in the flesh but in the Spirit, if in fact the Spirit of God dwells in you. Anyone who does not have the Spirit of Christ does not belong to him" (Rom 8:9 ESV).*

*"The same Spirit ... the same Lord ... but it is the same God who empowers them all in everyone" (1 Cor 12:4–6 ESV).*

*"The grace of the Lord Jesus Christ and the love of God and the fellowship of the Holy Spirit be with you all" (2 Cor 13:14 ESV).*

*"One Spirit ... one Lord ... one God and Father of all" (Eph 4:4–6).*

*"Chosen according to the foreknowledge of God the Father, by the sanctifying work of the Spirit, to obey Jesus Christ and be sprinkled with His blood" (1 Pet 1:1,2 NASB).*[2]

## God the Father

The Father is God. In fact, throughout the Bible, even for a new reader it is obvious that the "Father" is God or Yahweh himself. It is therefore not necessary to provide here many additional scriptural proofs of this truth.

"Father" appears approximately forty times in the Injil in clear reference to God (Rom 1:7; 1 Cor 1:3; 15:24; 2 Cor 1:2; Gal 1:1,3,4; Eph 1:2,17; 4:6; 5:20; 6:23; etc.).

When the name "God" appears in isolation, in general terms it refers to the person of the Father. "The Father" is the expression of the eternal and inaccessible God in his glory, totally different from any human conception or experience. At the same time it expresses the absolute source of all love and benefits for humankind. In many other verses, when God is mentioned together with the Son and the Holy Spirit, the reference is also to the Father, as we have previously seen. That is, in expressions such as "God, the Son, and the Holy Spirit" or "God, the Lord, and the Spirit," the reference to God is actually to the Father; and the Lord refers to the Son.

## God the Son

Verses that clearly affirm that the Son is God:

*"For to us a child is born ... and his name shall be called ... Mighty God, Everlasting Father" (Isa 9:6 ESV).*

*"Your God will come ... Then the eyes of the blind will be opened and the ears of the deaf will be unstopped" (Isa 34:4,5 NASB; cf. Matt 11:4–6).*

---

2   See also in the Injil: Luke 10:21,22; John 16:13–15; Acts 2:17–21; 5:30–32; 7:51–55; 10:38; 20:27,28; Romans 1:3,4; 5:5,6; 8:2,3,10,11; 15:30; 1 Corinthians 2:10–16; 2 Corinthians 3:3,17,18; Galatians 4:6; Ephesians 1:3–14; 2:18–22; 3:16–20; 2 Thessalonians 2:13,14; 1 Timothy 3:15,16; Titus 3:4–6; Hebrews 2:3,4; 9:14; 10:29–31; 1 Peter 4:14; Revelation 1:4,5.

*"A voice cries: 'In the wilderness prepare the way of the LORD; make straight in the desert a highway for our God ... And the glory of the LORD shall be revealed ... Behold your God!' ... Behold, the Lord GOD comes with might ... He will tend his flock like a shepherd"* (Isa 40:3–5,9–11 ESV).

*"I will raise up for David a righteous Branch, and he shall reign as king... And this is the name by which he will be called: 'The LORD is our righteousness'"* (Jer 23:5,6 ESV).

*"In the beginning was the Word, and the Word was with God, and the Word was God ... And the Word became flesh and dwelt among us"* (John 1:1,14 ESV).

*"Whatever the Father does, that the Son does likewise"* (John 5:19 ESV).

*"That all may honor the Son, just as they honor the Father. Whoever does not honor the Son does not honor the Father who sent him"* (John 5:23 ESV).

*"I [the Son] and the Father are one"* (John 10:30).

*"Thomas answered him [Jesus], 'My Lord and my God!'"* (John 20:28 ESV).

*"Christ himself was an Israelite as far as his human nature is concerned. And he is God, the one who rules over everything and is worthy of eternal praise!"* (Rom 9:5 NLT).

*"Christ Jesus, who, though he was in the form of God, did not count equality with God a thing to be grasped, but made himself nothing"* (Phil 2:5–7 ESV).

*"Our great God and Savior Jesus Christ"* (Titus 2:13 ESV).

*"But of the Son he says, 'Your throne, O God, is forever and ever'"* (Heb 1:8 ESV).

*"We are in him who is true, in his Son Jesus Christ. He is the true God and eternal life"* (1 John 5:20 ESV).

See also John 1:18; 5:18; Acts 20:28; 2 Corinthians 5:19; Colossians 1:19; 2:9; 1 Timothy 3:16; Hebrews 1; Revelation 1:8,17,18; 11:17; 15:3; 17:14.

When he came to the world, the Son took the form of a servant (a man). This is why in his humiliation he used expressions in which he appeared to consider God, and even angels, to be greater than himself (see Chapter 6). Some examples:

*"The Father is greater than I" (John 14:28).*

*"[He] did not count equality with God a thing to be grasped, but ... taking the form of a servant, being born in the likeness of men" (Phil 2:6–8 ESV).*

*"Having become [the Son] as much superior to angels ... we see him who for a little while was made lower than the angels, namely Jesus [the man] ... Therefore he had to be made like his brothers in every respect" (Heb 1:4; 2:9–17 ESV).*

## God the Holy Spirit

Finally, let us look at some verses that show the divinity of the Holy Spirit.

*"But the one who denies me before men will be denied before the angels of God ... the one who blasphemes against the Holy Spirit will not be forgiven" (Luke 12:9,10 ESV).*

The fact that the offence against the Holy Spirit cannot be forgiven, and thereby making salvation impossible for that person, makes it clear that this is an offense against God himself (cf. Heb 10:29).

*"Why has Satan filled your heart to lie to the Holy Spirit ... You have not lied to men but to God" (Acts 5:3,4 ESV).*

*"You, however, are not in the flesh but in the Spirit, if in fact the Spirit of God dwells in you. Anyone who does not have the Spirit of Christ does not belong to him" (Rom 8:9 ESV).*

*"Do you not know that you are God's temple [which means the same as:] and that God's Spirit dwells in you? ... Or do you not know that your body is a temple of the Holy Spirit within you, whom you have from God? You are not your own ... we are the temple of the Living God" (1 Cor 3:16; 6:19; 2 Cor 6:16 ESV, emphasis added).*

*"Now the Lord is the Spirit, and where the Spirit of the Lord is, there is freedom" (2 Cor 3:17 ESV).*

"The Spirit of Christ" is equivalent to "the Holy Spirit" (1 Pet 1:11,12; Rom 8:15; cf. Gal 4:16).

See also Matthew 12:28, with Exodus 8:19, 1 Corinthians 12:14, and Ephesians 4:4–6, or all the previously mentioned verses in which the Trinity is emphasized, or those where the Holy Spirit is named together with the Father and the Son.

The Holy Spirit is not merely a passive force, a simple reflection of divine action, like some people say. There are many biblical texts that leave no doubt as to the Holy Spirit's personality:

Blasphemy is an offense against the Holy Spirit (Matt 12:31; Heb 10:29). Only a personal being can be the object of an offense. Something inert, and even more a force, is indifferent to any verbal absurdity. No matter how much you curse a rock or a motor, it will never be considered an offense.

In the same way, the fact that the Holy Spirit can be lied to shows personality (see Acts 5:3).

Also, only a personal being can be a Helper and Comforter: John 14:26; 15:26; 16:17. And the same can be said for all the other expressions that indicate personality. The Holy Spirit:

- Speaks, announces: John 16:15; Acts 8:29; 10:19; 11:12,28; 13:2; 20:23; 21:4,11
- Decides, chooses: Acts 13:2,4; 15:28; 16:6; 20:28
- Pleads, thinks, and intercedes: Romans 8:27
- Bears witness: John 15:26; Acts 5:32
- Convicts: John 16:8
- Searches and knows: 1 Corinthians 2:10,11
- Is grieved: Ephesians 4:30
- Loves: Romans 5:5; etc.

## The Three Are One and the Same God

In the Holy Scriptures, each person of the Trinity is bestowed character-istics and attributes that are exclusive to Divinity:

|  | **Father** | **Son** | **Holy Spirit** |
|---|---|---|---|
| Eternity | Psalm 90:2 | Micah 5:2; Hebrews 7:2, 3 | Hebrews 9:14 |
| Omnipotence | Genesis 17:1 | Revelation 1:8 | Luke 1:35 |
| Omnipresence | Jeremiah 23:24 | Matthew 18:20; 28:20 | Psalm 139:7 |
| Omniscience | Jeremiah 19:10 | Colossians 2:3; Revelation 2:23 | 1 Corinthians 2:11 |
| Holiness | Revelation 15:4 | Luke 1:35; Acts 3:14; | His very name says it. |
| Truth | John 7:28 | Revelation 3:7 | 1 John 5:6 |
| Goodness | Romans 2:4 | Ephesians 5:25 | Nehemiah 9:20 |
| Fellowship | 1 John 1:3 | 1 John 1:3 | 2 Corinthians 13:14 |
| Immutability | James 1:17 | Hebrews 13:8 | Hebrews 9:14 |
| Inaccessibility | Romans 11:34 | Matthew 11:27 | Isaiah 40:13,14 |
| Creation | Psalm 102:25; Isaiah 44:24 | Proverbs 8:30; Colossians 1:16 | Genesis 1:2; Job 26:25 |
| Inspiration | 2 Timothy 3:16 | 1 Peter 1:10,11 | 2 Peter 1:21 |
| Resurrection | John 5:21 | John 5:21 | Romans 8:11 |
| Judgment | Romans 2:16 | John 5:22 | Isaiah 11:4 |
| Lordship | 1 Timothy 6:15,16 | Revelation 17:14 | 2 Corinthians 1:17 |

The three persons of the Trinity are worshiped by:

- Angels: Isaiah 6:3; Hebrews 1:6; Revelation 4:8; 5:8,11–17
- Humankind: Matthew 14:33; 28:9–17; Luke 24:51,52; John 9:38; 16:23,24; Ephesians 6:18
- In the doxologies: Numbers 6:24–26; 2 Corinthians 13:14

## The Three Persons Are Clearly Distinct

Each person in the Trinity participates fully in all of the divine attributes. God is present in all of his works as Father, Son, and Holy Spirit. Nonetheless, some works are assumed mainly by the Father, others by the Word, or both together. For example, the one who died on the cross was not the Father nor the Spirit but the Son. Likewise, there are activities assumed especially by the Holy Spirit. The following chart can help us see this:

| Father | Son | Holy Spirit |
|---|---|---|
| Transcendent | Imminent | Immanent |
| Being | Word | Action |
| Divinity | Lordship | Holiness |
| Origin | Mediator | Agent |
| Creator | Maker | Teacher |
| Revealer | Revelation | Inspiration |
| Promises | Fulfills | Guarantees |
| Justice | Judgment | Advocacy |
| Sentence | Suffers Sentence | Induces Repentance |
| Plan of Salvation | Sacrifice | Purification |
| Source of Love | Proof of Love | Pours out Love |
| Reconciliation | Redemption | Regeneration |
| Source of Life | Source of Resurrection | Resurrects the Believer |
| Merciful | Intercedes | Comforts |
| Power | Example | Equips |
| Almighty | Author of Miracles | Spiritual Power |
| Presence | Dwelling Place | Fullness |
| Corrects | Sustains | Disciplines |

# 5

## The Theological Approach

God, as regards his nature or substance (*wujud:* وُجُود, existence, being), is one and singular, from eternity past and throughout all eternity. No other but the one God exists.

God, as regards his identity (*dhat:* ذات, essence, selfness), has three clearly differentiated personalities. These are not simply different roles assumed by the Divinity, but three conscious centers that coexist in the one and only divine Being.

Each of these three persons is God himself and not parts of himself. The three participate fully in the same divine nature. As far as their "degree" of divinity, there is absolutely no difference between them whatsoever.

Each person possesses their own distinctive identity. The relationship between them is that of differentiated persons. The particularities and functions of each person are clearly defined and not confused with those of the others.

But the three—Father, Son, and Holy Spirit—are not three gods but the one and the same God.

In synthesis:

- God is one in nature.
- God exists in three persons.
- Each person is fully God.
- Each person has his own identity.
- The three persons are the one and same God.

Just as we see in the diagram, there is only one God. The Father is God, the Son is the same God, and so is the Holy Spirit. The three participate in the same being, but the persons are distinct. The Father is not the same person as the Son, the Son is not the same person as the Holy Spirit, and the Holy Spirit is not the same person as the Father. They are distinct from each other as regards their personhood. As regards their being, they are one and the same. This is the Trinity!

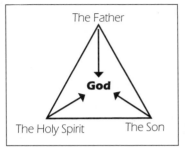

Figure 6

To use an expression similar to the one that Islamic theologians apply to the divine attributes: "The three persons of the Divinity are not the same as each other, but neither are they different from God."

It has been this way from eternity past. For this reason the triune God, from before time itself (Mic 5:2; 2 Tim 1:9; Heb 13:20), was able to make a covenant with himself—between the Father and the Son—to save humankind.

However, at this point, we need to clarify that the Trinity is not merely a way of appreciating the various functions of the Divinity. Nor are the persons of the Trinity different appearances that the transcendent God assumes in order to have contact with his creation, as if they were masks. On the other hand, it is true that God, in his relationship with humankind, undeniably acts as a triune God and with "different roles." This happens increasingly after sin enters the human race, and God seeks to save men and women. One divine Person judges, another dies in place of the sinner, and yet another one applies the value of this death to the believer. By the same token, once sin is vanquished and death is overcome in victory, the three persons of the Divinity will act on the same level: "When all things are subjected to him, then the Son himself will also be subjected to him who put all things in subjection under him, that God may be all in all" (1 Cor 15:25–28 ESV).

Everyone understands that God is one in essence. What is confusing is to say "there are three persons in God." Because from our perspective, which is temporal and material, we understand the word "person" to mean "individual." So let us explore this point further.

## What Does "Divine Person" Mean?

Let us consider first how Western theologians approach the terminology used. In the Council of Nicaea (AD 325), it was said that the Son is *Homoousion to Patri* (όμοούσιον τῷ Πατρί). That is, "of the same substance as the Father." What in some places have been called "conscious centers" or "differentiated identities" of divinity, Latin theologians gave expression to with the word "person," from the Greek word *prosopon*. *Prosopo* was the mask that Greek actors wore in their plays. These masks enabled the actor's voice to be projected with greater resonance; the words were "personated." The mask therefore acted like a loudspeaker.

The Greek theologians had their reservations regarding the use of this term because they did not want the persons of the Trinity to be understood as being mere appearances, as different masks that God would wear. They therefore used the word *hypostasis*, that is, "form of being or existing." The Arabic-Christian scholars in turn used the word *sifa* (صِفَة, quality, attribute, aspect) to express the persons of the Trinity. Or in other cases they adapted the Greek word *gnome* (γνώμη: intellect) to the Arabic *'aqnum* (أقنوم). But in Latin-based languages, and throughout Western theology, the expression that has won full acceptance and is the broadest in meaning is "person."

Today, we use the word "person" to simply refer to the conscious part of a man or woman, the part that thinks, decides, and feels. It constitutes character, identity, and individuality. But we must not confuse "person" with "human being." "Person" has to do with "the self" of each of us. It is the "I" that we also find in the definition that God gives of himself. "I AM" (Ex 3:14). God is not a man, a human, but he is a person, a conscious being.[1] If we consider possible synonyms of "person," we find words such as: being, individual, subject, personality, identity, character. But when we speak of the three persons in the Divinity we must make a major distinction. They are not three individuals or subjects (*ferd:* فرد, *fai'l:* فاعل). Rather, they are three personal identities (*dhat:* ذات,[2] *shakhs:* شخص).

---

1   God is not a person because he looks like us; rather it is us who have received God's personal condition.

2   According to *Webster's Online Dictionary, All Languages*, in Arabic "ذات" means: "self, essence, ego." In Farsi it means: "essence, person, hypostasis"; in Urdu, it means: "ego, entity, hypostasis."

"Individual" or "subject" expresses the unitary condition of the being or person. To speak of three individuals is to speak of three distinct beings. Whereas in the Trinity there are three persons in one single being, not three individuals. The "self," "I," or "person" is the conscious level of a being but is not its substance. For example, what makes women and men human is their nature—their body, morphology, aptitudes (ability to speak, to reason). Every woman and man, by definition, shares the same essential characteristics; if they did not they would not be humans. But as regards the person, every woman and man differs from everyone else in character, preferences, tastes, etc. Ali, Mehmet, and Murat are human beings by nature. Their natures are the same. However they are different persons. So, one thing is human nature and another is human person. In the same way, one thing is the divine nature and another the divine Person. Among human beings, one person coincides in one nature. Ali, Mehmet, and Murat are three individuals and three persons. In God, three persons coincide in one nature. The Trinity expresses the existence of three persons in a sole individual!

Therefore, the term "divine Person" does not refer to the divine Being or subject but to divine conscience, character, etc. The divine nature is one. However, the divine Persons—who are not individuals—do not form the divine nature (substance, attributes) but the divine personality (conscience, character, conduct). For that reason, when we speak of three persons we are not perforce speaking of three beings, because they are not three individuals.

It is my personality that enables me to speak of myself as "I." When we speak with or about someone we refer to "I," "you," or "him/her." But in God, "I," "you," and "him" coexist at the same time in a single being. They are not three gods, but neither a mere formulism. In the same way that I cannot say "I are coming,"—"I" is the first person singular and "are" is used for the second person; the roles of "I" and "you" should not be confused in a sentence—similarly, in the Trinity the roles of the Father, the Son, and the Spirit should not be confused. However, neither are they three distinct individuals. In humans, person and individual combine in a single being. But we must not forget that "person" is not a unique physical nature, limited to space, nor is it the unicity of the being but rather the uniqueness of its conscience, which does not occupy space.

Therefore the three persons of the Trinity are not three individuals, as if they were a committee of three. For example, to mention the confusing expression in the Qur'an, God is not "one of three" (Al-Ma'idah 5:73).

To what can the three persons of the Divinity be compared?

Let us imagine a theater play with three roles and a single actor. The actor interprets the characters successively. When one character speaks to the other characters, he speaks to distinct "persons" but at the same time speaks with himself, with the same actor. He asks a question and then, changing roles, gives the reply himself. But the one who asks and the one who replies are distinct characters. So we have a single actor (a single being) and three characters (three persons).

Of course God is neither an actor nor does he play a part; he is simply three persons in a single being. Furthermore, he is beyond time. Therefore, without needing to change roles or characters he is Father, Son, and Holy Spirit at the same time. His timeless condition can be likened to—and once again the example is inappropriate—the high speed that Superman uses to throw off his enemies. By changing locations at a speed higher than visual perception, to the amazement of the bad guys he can appear to be in three places at once. God does not change location at supersonic speed, because in the divine dimension there are no limitations such as speed, space, time, etc. God is in every place, at every moment. And he is also Father, Son, and Holy Spirit at every moment without detriment to his unicity!

## Theological Enunciation

The Trinity is a multidimensional topic. We cannot explain it in a linear form, and when we speak of its diverse aspects it might seem that we are speaking of different and even contradictory things. What am I saying by this? In the same way that when we represent the blueprint of an object we reduce its three dimensions to two—and we draw the different sides on separate pages as if they were different objects, when we define the triune structure of God—who surpasses the universe itself—we must do so with different approaches, which can give the sensation of being contradictory. But it is the only way of making the Trinity accessible to the limitations of our mind. The coexistence of several persons at once in a single being are not facts that contradict each other, rather they simply belong to a higher dimension.

The definition of one being and three persons in terms that are apparently mutually exclusive is nothing more than the attempt to reflect the different sides of the same fact. It reduces the "fourth" dimension of divinity to the three dimensions that as humans we are capable of assimilating. Having said this, we can define the Father, the Son, and the Holy Spirit in separate ways without forgetting that each person is the same God.

## God the Father

God is Father because:

- He is the source from which the *Kalam*—the Logos—emanates; in a spiritual sense he is the "progenitor" (Ps 2:7; Prov 8:22–24; John 1:14,18; 5:17–26; 8:54; 10:28–30; 14:12,13; Rom 8:29,32; Heb 1:1).

- At the same time he is the origin of all things, the Creator (Mal 2:10; Acts 17:28; 1 Cor 8:6; Eph 3:15; Heb 12:9; Jas 1:17).

- He is the Father who cares for the family of believers (Deut 32:6; Isa 63:16; 64:8; Jer 3:4; 31:9; Mal 1:6; Rom 11:29).

- He is the giver of spiritual life to every believer (Matt 5:45–48; 6:6–15; John 1:12,13; 3:3–8; 8:39–47; Rom 8:15–17; Gal 3:26; 2 Pet 1:4; 1 John 3:1).

"Father" expresses:

- The eternal, timeless, and glorious state of God, whom no one can nor will be able to see with their physical eyes (1 Tim 6:15,16; 2 Pet 3:8). He is the transcendent God.

- His condition of almighty, omnipresent, and omniscient God. He is the absolute God.

- He is the origin of all things: of the universe, of life, of love, of mercy, of grace, of judgment. He is the Creator, the beginning and end of everything.

How is the person of the Father differentiated from that of the Son or the Holy Spirit?

- The Father "begets" the Son—the Word emanates from him—and he "breathes" the Holy Spirit—the breath that emanates from his heart or essence.

- The person of the Father does not emanate from either of the other two persons.

- The Father, in the example of energy, constitutes the force. He is the "first" person of the Trinity. Being the first does not mean that he existed prior to the others but that he is the source and origin of everything. He is also the first person as regards to the order in which this mystery has been revealed to humanity. God first of all revealed himself as the transcendent and absolute God.

## God the Son

He is the *kalam* (word), *'ilm* (science), *hikmat* (wisdom) of God, the *Kalamu'llah* (divine Word), that is, the Logos or Word.

This Logos is being born uninterruptedly—is being generated—from eternity past in the bosom of the Father. And this is why it receives the name "Son" in the Bible.

The Logos is the revelation of the Father, the definition that God makes of himself. It is the "exegesis" (*tafsir:* تفسير) that is in the very bosom of God (see John 1:18). It is the concept that God has of himself; a living concept or definition and is therefore he himself.

The Logos is different from the person of the Father and has his own identity. In his pure state, God is all consciousness. And everything that emanates—not that which is created—from the divine Being is at the same time conscious. Nothing "unconscious" exists in God; for example, like in humans, for example, the insensitive parts of the body: nails or hair. Therefore, the Logos that originates in God's "interior" and which he makes known to the "exterior" is also self-aware. When the Logos says, "God is like this or like that," he differentiates himself as a second person by speaking of God as "he" or "him." Thus it is God himself but a different person—the person of the Son.

That which in the Son comes from the Father is not his divine substance—because both are of the same substance—but his personhood.

The "birth" of the Son is not a creation, nor is it either procreation; it is a generation, a spiritual act. It occurs from eternity past (Prov 8:22,23). To create something implies that it previously did not exist and now it does. But where time does not exist—in eternity—there is no "before" or "after." We therefore cannot speak of a "first" generation of the Logos, nor can we correctly state "prior to his existence" or "after being begotten." The divine Logos is as eternal as God, because he is God and has not been created!

Therefore, the Logos possesses his own identity in the bosom or heart of God. He is generated—he emanates—"uninterruptedly" from eternity past and "at the same time"; from the same eternity he possesses the fullness of his personhood.

The Son is like the mirror or monitor that reflects the Father. In the Bible, the glory of God that shines in Christ is compared to the reflection from a mirror (2 Cor 3:18).

The Logos reveals the Father fully. He is the revelation in person. The "preserved tablet" (*lawhin mahfuzin:* لَوْح مَحْفُوظ) expressed in the Qur'an, is interpreted in Islam as the tablets that contain the eternal word of God in heaven (Al-Buruj 85:21,22). But it is the Logos who is truly in heaven from all eternity as the Word of God. The Word that lives in the divine heart is not a collection of tablets but the very essence of all that God reveals and expresses: the *kalam nafsi*. The Bible—the *kalam lafzi*—constitutes only some of the expressions of this Logos. On the other hand, Jesus is the full expression of the Logos!

The Son is at the same time mediator between the Creator and the creation. This is similar to how words are the bridge between the speaker and the hearer. God has created everything through the "mediation" of his Son (John 1:3; Col 1:16; Heb 1:2).

The Logos, the very definition of the Divinity and the expression of its fullness, entered our world two thousand years ago incarnated into human nature. In this way, the invisible nature of God is made visible perfectly in the life and person of Jesus Christ (John 1:18; 14:9; 2 Cor 4:4; Col 1:15; Heb 1:3).

In the energy example, the Logos is the light. He is the Second Person of the Trinity. This does not express degree nor category but rather his function within the Divinity.

# God the Holy Spirit

The Arabic word for "spirit" (*ruh:* روح) comes from the Hebrew *ruach* (רוּחַ). The Hebrew and the Greek (*pneuma:* πνευμα) expressions have the same meanings: wind, blow, breath, air current, and emanation.

The wind is a force capable of moving objects. The Spirit is the divine force that gives shape to, initiates change, puts into movement, leads to order, and moves hearts so they will have the desire to please God.

In eternity, the Spirit is the "connecting line" for the flow of love between the Father and the Son. As in the illustration of energy, which gives off heat in its transformation from power to light and vice versa, the Holy Spirit is like "waves" of love that the Father and the Son pour out in their reciprocal relationship (Rom 5:5). It is like the sparks that fly out when a welding electrode comes into contact with metal.

Within the relationships of the Divinity, the Spirit proceeds from the Father and from the Son by way of love: "proceeds from the Father" and is the Spirit of truth of whom Christ said, "I will send to you" (John 15:26). He is therefore "the Spirit of the Lord" (Acts 5:9; 2 Cor 3:17) and also "the Spirit of Christ" (Rom 8:9).

The Spirit receives the name of "Holy." This does not mean that the other two persons of the Trinity are not holy, because "Holy, holy, holy is the LORD of hosts; the whole earth is full of his glory!" (Isa 6:3). Father, Son, and Holy Spirit are the three times holy God. And it is the Spirit who in a special way receives the name "holy" because it is he who separates women and men and causes them to turn to God—indeed the word "holy" in Hebrew means "something or someone separated for God's service." It is also the Holy Spirit who produces the new birth in the believer (John 3:3,5,8), seals the believer (Eph 1:13), sanctifies the believer (2 Thess 2:13), and equips the believer.

In John 14:26, 15:26, and 16:7 the Holy Spirit is given the Greek word *parakletos* (Paraclete), which means Advocate, Defender, Helper, Comforter, Counselor, Pleader. In some circles, Muslim scholars try to demonstrate that the New Testament predicts the coming of the Islamic Prophet. For this purpose they reinterpret the term "paraclete" to say that the Injil announces the coming of Muhammad. The argument presented is that "paraclete" means "the praised one," and "praise" in Arabic is *hamd* (حمد), which is the root of *Muhammad* (محمد) as well. However, in Greek "the one who is praised" would not be *parakletos* but rather *perikletos*. Besides, it is made quite clear in the verses in John that the *parakletos* is none other than the Spirit of Christ.[3]

The *Ruhu'l-Qudus* (رُوحُ الْقُدُس, Holy Spirit) mentioned in the Qur'an, where the virginal conception of Jesus in Mary is told, is generally interpreted by Islam as referring to the angel Gabriel. But in Luke, in the Injil, for example, Gabriel clearly makes reference to the Holy Spirit as someone completely distinct from him (Luke 1:35).

God, in his eternal state is all energy and pure conscience. In his transcendent state he does not establish direct contact with the world, particularly after sin entered the universe. The transcendence of God and the nontranscendent world are incompatible. They cannot enter into contact with each other "as they are"; that is, the finite and the infinite, the holy and the unholy cannot mix. God's contact with the world occurs through his "connecting line," the Holy Spirit. He is the immanent God.

It is the Word—the Son—who facilitates *communication* with the world, but it is the Holy Spirit who makes *contact* possible with the world. The light shines around us, from the outside. The heat, however, penetrates and transforms us inside. The Logos incarnated in Jesus reveals the Father, and the Holy Spirit "incarnated" in the believer molds the desire of the Father and the image of Jesus in the believer. The one who makes possible contact between God and our spirit is God the Holy Spirit. The Father is God in his transcendent state, the Son is the imminent God who enters the world as man, and the Holy Spirit is the immanent God who is active *within* creation itself.

---

3   The Holy Spirit is the other Comforter, that is, the continuator of Christ himself. In fact, the Comforter was among the disciples (in the person of Jesus; see 1 John 2:1), it is announced that he would live in them after Jesus' departure from earth, and that with the Spirit's coming he would abide with all believers at the same time until the end of the world (John 14:16,17). It is Jesus who sends the Comforter (John 15:26), and therefore he wanted the disciples to await the coming of the Spirit (which occurred a few days later—Acts 1:24; 2:1–4), and lastly, the Paraclete is spirit, without body. From all this it is very clear that the Paraclete has nothing to do with Muhammad but that he is the Third Person of the Trinity—pure Spirit and God himself!

Consequently, the Spirit is in charge of applying the will of God and the effects of divine revelation, expiation, and intercession within the believer. This idea is seen in the dialogue between the Father and the Son in John 16:13–15. The Spirit repeats the dialogue of the Eternal One within the believer; that is, he imparts the divine life by taking what is of the Son—which is to also take from the Father—and communicates it to the believer's spirit.

The Holy Spirit, in the act of communicating God's words and life to the believer, is revealed as the Third Person in the Trinity. He is love in action. And this movement of God's love has consciousness in itself. Finally, the "I" (Father), the "you" (Son), and the "he" (Holy Spirit) that coinhabit the Divinity are clearly defined.

The Son is the Word that emanates from the bosom or heart of the Father and the Holy Spirit is the flow of love between Father and Son. As a result, people perceive the Logos as the "expression" of truth and the Spirit as the "impression" of love, or like the imprint that is left on the human heart.

On the other hand, the Spirit reminds and teaches the truths proclaimed by Jesus Christ (John 16:13); intercedes for the saints, that is, for every believer (Rom 8:27); and apportions gifts according to his will (1 Cor 12:11). He is the divine Person who applies the power of God in the life of the believer!

The Spirit is at the same time the *agent* or *channel* who applies revelation, salvation, justification, the new birth, redemption, new creation—the divine image—and more works of God in the life of the believer. The Father is the *designer* and *origin* of all of these, and the Son is the *executor* and *means*. For example, in 1 Corinthians 1:30 and 6:11 it says that by the initiative (origin) of the Father we have been given wisdom, justification, sanctification, and redemption. These are not mere scattered virtues but qualities that belong to Jesus Christ himself (means); that is, the Spirit (agent) stamps on our hearts these values that in essence are Christ himself.

In the example of energy, the Spirit is the heat generated. This is how we have known the Third Person of the Trinity. The fact of enumerating the divine Persons corresponds to the order in which they proceed or emanate one from the other in eternity. The person of the Father does not proceed from any other person, the Son is like the "voice" of the Father, and the Spirit is the "breath" of the Father and the Son.[4]

## Relationship between the Three Divine Persons

We have illustrated the Father as divine thought, the Son as divine Word, and the Spirit as divine action. In a person, thought, word, and action are manifestations or expressions of one individual. But from the point of view of their origin, whereas the word and the action originate in the mind, they do not shape or mold the thought. An individual's movements come from the decisions made in the mind in terms such as: "I am going to do this or that." But the individual's actions do not produce his or her thoughts or words (see Figure 7).

Similarly, at the same time that Father, Son, and Holy Spirit are personal expressions of the one and only God, the Father is the source par excellence, the Son is the constant means, and the Holy Spirit the absolute end. From the point of view of who "generates" whom, the Father engenders the Word and breathes the Spirit. But neither the Son nor the Holy Spirit gives origin to the Father. The Son comes from the Father and on the other hand sends the Spirit. The Son is the mediator. The Holy Spirit is breathed by the Father and sent by the Son, but he does not give origin to the Father or the Son. He is the receiver par excellence in this current of life that flows in the heart of the Divinity.

But, as we have been reminded above, the source neither empties itself, nor does the current die, nor does the "vital fluid" become stagnated in the end. It is not a flow that diminishes or runs out. It would look like those decorative lava lamps, filled with bright colors that flow continuously from one concavity to the last one without the liquid dwindling at the origin or

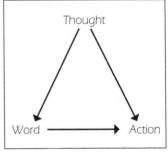

Figure 7

---

4    But this Father-Son-Holy Spirit flow is not a succession of source-channel-pool, where the source empties itself, the flow ceases, the reservoir fills, and there is an irremediable running out or diminishing.

increasing at the end. The Father (the source) lives in the fullness of divinity, and the same thing happens with the Son (the channel) and with the Holy Spirit (the destination).

At the same time that they participate of an entire and single divine nature and all of its attributes, each of the three persons of the Trinity shows their own peculiar and distinguishing behavior in every divine activity. For example:

In the act of creation (Gen 1:1–3; 2:7; Job 26:13), as designer the Father says "be" (source, origin), the Son is the creative Word (means or mediator), and the Spirit, who gives shape to the material and gives it life (agent), is comparable to the hands of a potter who shapes the clay (Job 10:8 with 33:6; Psalm 119:73).

In the act of revelation (Heb 1:1,2; 1 Pet 1:10–12; 2 Pet 1:21), God the Father reveals the divine mysteries (source, origin), the Son expresses the revealed truth (means, author), and the Spirit inspires the minds of the prophets (conducting agent).

In 1 Peter 1:2, the Father plans salvation according to his foreknowledge (source, origin), Jesus Christ makes it possible through his death on the cross (means or executor), and the Holy Spirit applies the value of the blood, "sprinkling" the life of the believer and sanctifying him or her (supplier agent).

From John 6:27, Romans 8:29, and Ephesians 1:13 it is clear that the Father seals the heart of the believer (source, origin), seals it with the impression or likeness of the Son (means, image), through the action of the Holy Spirit who is the seal itself (agent, instrument).

In prayer (John 14:13,14; Rom 8:26,27; Heb 7:25), as the one we address, the Father is the reason for the prayer (source, origin), the Son empowers the prayer so it reaches its destination (means and endorser), and the Holy Spirit strengthens the prayer with unspeakable groanings from the believer's heart (intercessory agent).

In 1 Corinthians 12:4–6, the Father is manifested as the source of power (origin), the Son distributes the varieties of service as Lord (mediator), and the Holy Spirit applies grace inside each of us in the form of spiritual abilities (equipping agent).

When he corrects his people or an individual (Gen 6:3; Isa 63:9,10; Luke 22:32; Heb 12:5–9), the Father suffers our rebellions and decides the discipline to apply (source, origin), the Son gives us strength through his intercession that we might come out from our trials victorious (mediator, strengthener), and the Holy Spirit applies the correction and contends with people (executor, agent).

Lastly, in 2 Corinthians 13:14 the Father is the source of love (origin), the Son (means and mediator) brings us his strength in the form of undeserved grace, and the Holy Spirit makes possible the contact and fellowship with that love (conducting agent).

These manifestations of God—his invisible being, his revelation as living Word, and his Spirit of power—are something more than mere attributes or forms of the Divinity. They are three persons, equal to God but distinct among them. The Trinity clarifies the bond between the transcendent God (the Father), the imminent God (the Son), and the immanent God (the Holy Spirit). All this is not a series of mere theological formulisms devoid of all life and practical application, but the understanding of God who comes out to meet us as the source of life in himself—as Father, as the precursor of life in his mediation—as Son, and who imparts that life to everyone in his "immersion" in the world—as Holy Spirit.

The Trinity defines the internal constitution of God, who, as three persons, imparts life from eternity, within time and within creation itself!

# 6

## The Incarnation[1]

*"God was manifested in the flesh" (1 Tim 3:16 NKJV).*

The word "incarnation" means "to become embodied" by way of a birth. On the other hand, the word "reincarnation," which comes from the same root, means to "become embodied again" through birth. Both words express the physical embodiment of a spirit being. But "incarnation" refers to a first and unique body, whereas the idea of "reincarnation" is that a spirit that has already had a previous corporeal life can exist bodily again—two, three, or more times. (The Holy Scriptures do not accommodate such a concept. See Hebrews 9:27.)

By definition, incarnation is the exclusive prerogative of the Word. And it not only implies acquiring a body but acquiring a complete human nature. In addition to the text quoted at the start of this chapter, the Bible also expresses the incarnation thus: "And the Word became flesh and dwelt among us" (John 1:14).

Since Jesus Christ is the center of the Christian life and faith, the emphasis given to correctly knowing his exact nature can never be stressed enough. Whether or not we benefit from his salvation and from his ministry of

---

1　This chapter on the incarnation has been devised in response to some of the arguments of Western origin, of which certain critics in Turkey also make use of to attack the doctrine. For this reason, aside from an exposition properly addressing the Muslim mind, it will be helpful to expose some doctrinal bases as the systematic theology of the West raises them. However, considering the Muslim theological criteria, there are two things to be taken into account and briefly explained: The first is the Muslim argument that it is "impossible" for God to become incarnate. The second is the concept of *tanzil*, namely that the Qur'anic revelation comes down.

intercession on our behalf depends on this vital issue. It is not enough to accept Jesus only as a prophet. We must accept him as he really is!

Muslims are taught that God is infinite and that he could not become finite; and we as Christians agree with this. On the other side, according to Christianity as well as to Islam, God can do anything he wants. If God decides to participate in human experience at a certain level, it does not necessarily mean that he will stop being divine. Because what is incarnate in Jesus wasn't the divine substance—*wujud*, but it was his divine identity—the *dhat* of the *kalam nafsi*. We believe, as Muslims do, that it is "impossible" for God to become human in the sense of altering, limiting, or losing his divine nature.

When we as Christians say that God became human in Jesus Christ, we must not think that his incarnation takes dignity away from God's magnificence. As we will see, even when Jesus Christ is the Word of God incarnate and the whole fullness of the Deity dwells in him (Col 2:9), his humanity does not participate directly of the divine substance. That is, his humanity does not become deified in the incarnation, nor does his divinity become humanized. Rather, his divinity becomes installed in a human nature in such a way that the two natures do not become mixed or fused together, and yet both natures remain inseparably joined in the person of the Son—the *kalam nafsi*. And this is the reason why God provided human nature through the virginal birth and blew the Word into Mary's womb through the Holy Spirit: so his essence would not be contaminated by the stain of inherited sin or limited to human substance. In Jesus, God did not contaminate himself with the "soot" of creation, in the same way that a chimney sweep doesn't get his or her hands dirty when cleaning a chimney by wearing gloves.

"Incarnation" is the term that expresses the process by which the eternal and living Word of God—the *kalam nafsi*—could enter into the universe in a human body, similarly as God had sent before his word into books, which are bodies as well. Does not the infinite word of Allah come into contact with the finite world in the holy books—that is, the limitations of the physical form and our ability to read and understand it? Since this is so, why cannot the Word of God become flesh—as the Bible says? Why cannot an emanation of God (his word) take a physical form (holy book) or even a human form (Jesus)—since God can do anything?

The very Injil—the Gospel—that descended from heaven is Jesus himself; the living Word, incarnated as a living book (see John 1:1,14; 3:13,31). The Qur'an speaks of Jesus as having received *tanzil*: revelation from God; where *tanzil* means "to come down from heaven."[2] It has been suggested even by some Islamic scholars that the *tanzil* of Christianity—what descended from heaven—is the person of Jesus himself.[3] Such as John 3:13 says about him: "No one has gone up to heaven except the one who came down[4] from heaven, the Son of Man who is in heaven." Therefore the incarnation may be defined as the *tanzil* of the *kalam nafsi* into a human nature.

Let's see how this truth was revealed throughout the centuries.

Already in the Taurat (Gen 3:15) it was announced that one would be born of the seed of woman (cf. Gal 4:4) who would crush the head of the serpent (Satan, the devil or evil one). In Genesis 12:3 the genealogical line is defined even more specifically regarding this one to be born, specifying that he would come from the seed of Abraham (cf. Gal 3:8,16). Likewise, in Genesis 49:10 it was prophesied that: "The scepter shall not depart from Judah, nor the ruler's staff from between his feet, until Shiloh comes." This announces beforehand the royal line of Judah from which would come the Messiah. In the Zabur, Psalms 2, 22, 45, and 110 are also explicitly related to the Messiah. In these Psalms it speaks of the awaited Messiah as the "Son of God," "God," and "Lord"!

In the Prophets, and specifically in Isaiah 7:14, the Messiah is mentioned with the name "Immanuel," which means "God with us." In Isaiah 9:6 and 11:1–5 he is clearly mentioned as God, with the title of Messiah, and it is announced that he will come filled with the Holy Spirit. Isaiah 53 narrates his suffering, his death, and his resurrection, and Isaiah 61:1–3 presents the Gospel (Injil) of salvation or the complete redemption of humankind. Likewise, Jeremiah 23:5,6 and 33:14–17 speak of the future justice that the Messiah would bring. Whereas in Daniel 7:13 it speaks of the Messiah as the "son of man," and in Daniel 9:24–27 gives the exact

---

2 For instance see Al 'Imran 3:65 (*unzilati'l-tauratu wa'l-injilu:* أُنْزِلَتِ التَّوْرَاةُ وَالْإِنْجِيلُ), which literally means "The Torah and the Gospel were brought down."

3 Cyril Glassé, *The New Encyclopedia of Islam* (Lanham, MD: AltaMira Press, 2002), 383.

4 In the Arabic version, *nazal:* نَزَلَ (bring down, come down), which constitutes the root of *tanzil:* تَنْزِل (descent, downfall). From which comes the word that the Qur'an uses to indicate the revelations given to Muhammad as well as those given to the previous prophets: *unzile:* أُنْزِلَ (Al-Baqarah 2:4).

day of his execution. Haggai 2:7 says that then "the desired of all nations will come," and the temple will be filled with glory. To Zechariah (9:9) it is revealed that the Savior would arrive riding on a donkey's colt (cf. Matt 21:5 and John 12:15). Finally, Malachi speaks of the prophet that would come as the precursor of the Messiah (that is, John the Baptist; Mal 3:1).

The prophetic writings contain some three hundred predictions concerning the Messiah, similar to those quoted earlier. They were revealed hundreds of years before his coming and were faithfully fulfilled in his earthly life. And among all of them are very clear references to his supernatural identity.

This is why the doctrine of the incarnation is much more than a simple doctrine; it proclaims the corporeal coming to the world of the Word filled with the Spirit. This was planned by God from eternity past and meticulously prepared for throughout history. Said differently, the prophets and the Holy Scriptures were instruments in preparing the coming of the Messiah. Christ was the seal of God's eternal plan. That is: all the prophets and all written revelation direct us towards Jesus Christ. And he is the focus towards whom they all point! Why did God plan to send the Messiah, his incarnate Word? Because God, who is love, wanted to give salvation to each of us in spite of our rebellion against him! The Messiah is the Savior of the world!

The value of the sacrifice on the cross and the eternal salvation of every person required the unique person of the Messiah to have a double nature (that is, he would share both the divine and human nature). Only someone human, like us, could represent us or take our place as our expiation. And only by being God at the same time in his person could he offer universal salvation through his death, because then his sacrifice had an infinite value (John 12:27; Acts 3:18; Eph 2:16–18; Heb 2:11–18; 4:15; 7:26,28; 9:22; 1 Pet 1:19; 1 John 2:3).

Upon opening the Injil, the first thing we find is a list of the genealogies of Jesus Christ (Matt 1:1–17). The list in Luke goes all the way back to Adam. This ratifies the historical roots of the Injil and the fulfillment of the predictions about Jesus Christ in the Old Testament. At the same time it is emphasized that the announced Messiah, in spite of his supernatural nature, was a human being like us (except that he was sinless).

Therefore Jesus, the Son of God, shares two natures—the divine and the human—in a single person. Even though some people have erred in interpreting this truth, the Holy Scriptures proclaim it with exceptional balance. The most relevant declaration from Scripture is Philippians 2:5–8 (ESV): "Christ Jesus ... though he was in the form of God, did not count equality with God a thing to be grasped, but made himself nothing, taking the form of a servant, being born in the likeness of men. And being found in human form, he humbled himself by becoming obedient to the point of death, even death on a cross."

Let us define a little more some of the most significant expressions in the original Greek of this text: "Christ Jesus ... though he was in the form of God ... took the form of a servant" (that is, of a man). The Greek word for the twice-mentioned "form" is *morphos*.

The word *morphos*, translated as "form," expressed in Greek the substance of a being; that is, the essence of a person. So when it repeats "though he was in the form of God" and then "took the form of a servant," it means that he participated in the divine "substance" as well as in the human.

In his eternal state as divine Word, Jesus Christ had the nature of God, which corresponded to him as such—and of course he still has that nature today because he was God and he is God. The expressions "was in the form of" and "did not count equality with God a thing to be grasped" are interpreted in some circles to mean that Jesus never dared to usurp the divine nature, as if it did not correspond to him. However the Greek is very clear: "existing [*huparchon*] in the form of God." He already possessed the divine "substance" and existed as such. The verb form denotes a continuous state. Anything that continues its existence was already like that previously. The Son was God prior to becoming a man, and after clothing himself with a human nature, still "maintained his existence as God." That is, his essence was the divine Being.

But this Being left aside his rights—he stripped himself of his glory. Even though in essence, character, and holiness he was God, he chose to live under the same conditions as any human being, without taking advantage of his divine attributes. It would be somewhat like Aladdin fighting Jaffar between palace columns without making use of his flying carpet. Jesus Christ did not use his divinity to his advantage in order to make his life easier to bear. He conditioned himself to think, feel, decide, and live as any human being: "Christ Jesus ... made himself nothing." But this life was the life of a man whose person—identity and character—was and is God!

In principle, everyone who accepts that Jesus is sent from God, whether the person is a Christian or not, also accepts the truth that Jesus is a supernatural envoy. That is, a supernatural nature was incarnated in Jesus, evidenced in the virginal conception of Mary. Jesus is the divine Word that entered the sphere of human life through his corporal birth. Therefore, on the one hand there is a human nature that began with the conception in the Virgin Mary's womb and the corporal birth; and on the other hand there is a spiritual nature preexistent to the birth. The resulting discussion revolves around the following: Is this spiritual being, called the divine Word (or *Kalamu'llah*), God himself, or is he a distinct and separate being?

Only the Bible can respond categorically to this question. However, certain circles alien to Christianity, as well as some dissident cults within Christianity, affirm that, according to the Holy Scriptures, the Word incarnate in Jesus is a different being from God.

According to them, the Word (the Son of God, the divine Word or the *Kalimat'ullahi*):

- Was created. Some people go as far as to say he was the first angel to be created and that everything else was then created by him.

- Therefore he is not eternal (*qadim*); nor is he all powerful.

- According to these interpretations, Jesus never claimed to be God.

- And neither did the apostles believe that Jesus was God.

- When Jesus invokes the name of God or makes reference to him—they add—he refers to someone different from himself.

- They also affirm things such as that Jesus was a divinity but was not Yahweh or Jehovah (that is, the personal name of the only and absolute God).

There have been people throughout history who have not understood correctly the Bible's declarations about God and Jesus and that various interpretations have arisen from the subject. However, this has happened because they have gone to the Scriptures with preconceived ideas. Instead of accepting the revealed truths just as they are declared, they accept only that which the finite human mind can understand to be true. And thus the human mind becomes the absolute judge of what is true and what is false. Consequently, they reject Jesus' divinity a priori and only emphasize the biblical references to his humanity. They ignore the passages that speak unequivocally about Jesus' divinity, saying that the texts have been altered or they force another interpretation. But this eludes the evidence!

To say that the Holy Scriptures have been altered or manipulated is an offense against God, who has promised to protect them from error. On the other hand, to distort their meaning is to fall into heresy. When analyzing the Holy Scriptures, we must distinguish "unequivocal declarations" from those that admit various interpretations.

At the same time we must distinguish between what the text says in and of itself and the conclusions that we may reach. Especially if our conclusions categorically affirm concepts that are not explicitly expressed in the text. For example, the Bible clearly says in several passages that Jesus is God (see Chapter 4, section d). But in their interpretation of other passages, some people reach the conclusion that Jesus is not God. However, none of these latter passages state explicitly that Jesus is not God, and there are also texts that allow for varying interpretations.

Once these two rudimentary principles have been established regarding the interpretation of biblical texts,[5] let us see what the Scriptures affirm regarding the seven objections to the divinity of Christ mentioned earlier.

## The Logos Is Uncreated

The Logos cannot be created or be a creature because the Injil clearly says that "through him all things were made; without him nothing was made that has been made" (John 1:3). The words "all things" and "nothing" are

---

5    We are not entering here into deeper and more relevant hermeneutical details; rather we are merely trying to capture what the text says. The doctrine of the divinity of Christ is a truth interwoven with many textual references, but in this analysis our starting point is that all of the biblical texts have equal authoritative value. We do not accept the pretensions of liberal criticism that interprets certain texts capriciously, not by what they say but as texts added subsequently to the biblical text. According to this line of interpretation, the doctrine of the divinity of Christ is not conditioned by the biblical text; rather, the biblical text is conditioned by the held doctrine of the Divinity. This is nothing else than giving support to those sectors of Islam that say that the Bible has been adulterated.

conclusive, so we therefore cannot include the Logos among the things that were created. God does not use means nor instruments beyond his attributes to create; he never uses other creatures: "This is what the LORD says—your Redeemer, who formed you in the womb: I am the LORD, who has made *all things*, who alone stretched out the heavens, who spread out the earth *by myself*" (Isa 44:24, emphasis added). The creative Word is not an instrument separate from the Divinity.

In Colossians 1:15, the phrase "the firstborn over all creation" is used, referring to Jesus. Based on this expression, some people maintain that the Son was the first created being. However, the word "firstborn" has two possible meanings in biblical culture: 1) the first son to be born into a household, and 2) the heir by right of the family heritage. This second meaning gives us to understand that "the firstborn over all creation" does not necessarily mean "the first created being." In fact, Jacob, even though he was not the firstborn, was able to buy the birthright (Gen 25:31–33). This way, Jacob *was able to be the firstborn without having been born first*. If we consider the name Atatürk based on its etymology,[6] we would understand that every Turkish citizen is joined in blood relationship to him. But we know perfectly well that Atatürk has a symbolic meaning, which is used as an honorific title. Likewise here, the expression "firstborn" has a symbolic meaning and is used as an honorific title.

On what criteria do we base our decision to choose the second meaning of "firstborn"? According to the criteria of the text. Let's take a look at it. In the same passage of Colossians 1, in verse 18, the term "firstborn" is used once again in reference to the resurrection of Christ. Here the expression does not convey the meaning that he was the first to resurrect, because long before Christ we already find examples of resurrection in the Scriptures: in the time of the prophet Elijah (1 Kgs 17:17–24), Elisha (2 Kgs 4:32–35), Lazarus (John 11), and the dead that rose at the moment of Christ's death (Matt 27:52,53), just to mention a few. "Firstborn" in Colossians *is not an expression of order but of degree*; it does not mean the first in the list, but the most important. It is an expression of the preeminence of Christ! Therefore, in the passage we are considering,

---

6   Ataturk is the honorary name received by Mustafa Kemal, the founder of the Republic of Turkey (1923) and means "Father of the Turks."

"firstborn" does not mean either "the first to be born" or "the first to be resurrected." It follows, then, that neither can we assign to it the meaning of "the first created being."

What's more, in the same chapter of Colossians, in the remaining verses between 15 and 18, this possibility can be categorically rejected, for it says: "For by him [by the Son] all things were created: things in heaven and on earth, visible and invisible, whether thrones or powers or rulers or authorities; all things were created by him and for him. He is before all things, and in him all things hold together" (verses 16 and 17). Now, could he have created himself? Is it possible that another separate being, also equally eternal, exists prior to him who "is before all things"? The answer is self-evident. We cannot substitute that which seems "implicit" to us for that which is "explicit" in the text. The expressions "first created being" and "firstborn" are, in fact, two terms that, from the outset, have nothing in common with each other. What's more, "firstborn" refers here to the title given to an heir, to the head of a clan, to the one who will give his family name to the ensuing dynasty. When the title "firstborn" is applied to the Son, no allusion is being made to his origin but to the fact that *he is the origin* of all things! When "firstborn" is used in relation to Christ's resurrection, it is not because the Son has been the first to resurrect, but because *he is the source* of all resurrection!

In a similar way, the Greek expression *he arche tes ktiseos tou theou* is used in Revelation 3:14 in reference to the Son of God; that is, "the beginning of the creation of God" (NASB). This expression can be understood in two ways: a) the first of all creation, or b) of the origin creation (that is, the Creator). Just as in Turkish and in English, the Greek work *arche* can equally mean "first" or "origin"; both definitions (a and b) can be considered correct. However, in the light of the unequivocal declarations of the Scriptures regarding the creative role of the Son, the second definition (b) is obviously the correct one. The Son is not the first creature but the Creator who has given origin to all things. There is no margin of error! Because we cannot subordinate the clear affirmation made in Scripture—such as the Son has created all things—to the interpretation we give to expressions susceptible to various definitions—such as "first created being" or "origin of creation."

## The Logos Is Eternal

If the Logos were not eternal, we would suppose that, prior to the act of creation, God lacked word or wisdom. Is this compatible with the concept of divinity? There is nothing in the Bible affirming that "the Son of God is not eternal," whereas there are many other affirmations that openly declare that he is indeed eternal: "I was appointed from eternity, from the beginning, before the world began" (Prov 8:23); "[his] origins are from of old, from ancient times" (Mic 5:2); "He is before all things" (Col 1:17); "without beginning of days or end of life" (Heb 7:3); "Jesus Christ is the same yesterday and today and forever" (Heb 13:8). And so we could continue. Clearly, we cannot subordinate passages like those mentioned here to personal conclusions that lack specific Scriptural support.

## The Logos Is the Almighty

Another objection is that the Logos is not the All Powerful God but rather an inferior divinity. But what does the Bible declare? "I am the Alpha and the Omega," says the Lord God, "who is, and who was, and who is to come, the Almighty" (Rev 1:8). Who is the one "who is to come"? The Messiah (Rev 1:7). This same verse 7 says, "Look, he is coming with the clouds," and it is understood that the one "who is to come" refers to the second coming of Christ to earth. And, who is "the Alpha and the Omega"? Once again, it is the Messiah (see Rev 21:6; 22:13). We cannot subordinate clear statements in the Bible to preconceived ideas. The one who will come to earth a second time is "the Almighty"!

## Jesus Said He Was God

Is there a clear statement anywhere by Jesus regarding his divinity? Let's consider several. "I [the Son] and the Father are one" (John 10:30); "Anyone who has seen me has seen the Father ... I am in the Father and the Father is in me" (John 14:9–11). "Jesus said to them, 'My Father is always at his work to this very day, and I, too, am working' ... he was even calling God his own Father, making himself equal with God"

(John 5:17,18).[7] "It is not for a good work that we are going to stone you but for blasphemy, because you, being a man, make yourself God" (John 10:33 ESV). Here the meaning for the Jews of the expression "God is my Father" is emphasized. We must not forget that Jesus was also a Jew. He knew perfectly well how his coreligionists would interpret this phrase! Once more we must acknowledge the biblical evidence and conclude that Jesus did affirm his divinity.

There are also many other passages that we could analyze, such as: "Unless you believe that I AM—Yahweh—you will die in your sins" (John 8:24,28); or also, "For the Son of Man is Lord of the Sabbath" (Matt 12:8); and "What do you think about the Christ? ... David ... calls him 'Lord'? For he says, 'The Lord said to my Lord'" (Matt 22:41–45). And in many other expressions similar to these, Christ applies to himself the lordship, attributes, and prerogatives that correspond to the one and only God!

## The Apostles Said Jesus Is God

Did the apostles ever affirm that Jesus was God? Thomas said so quite clearly: "My Lord and my God" (John 20:28); and also Paul: "Christ, who is God over all, forever praised! Amen" (Rom 9:5); "Who (Christ Jesus), being in the form of God" (Phil 2:6); "our great God and Savior, Jesus Christ" (Titus 2:13); while John says that "He (the Son) is the true God and eternal life" (1 John 5:20) to quote just a few verses. Once again we return to the same point: passages or expressions with an ambiguous meaning—which we will also deal with—do not deny the meaning of declarations such as these that are completely unequivocal. It is quite clear that the apostles affirm in many places that the Son is God, whereas in no place do they state that he is not God—which would be absurd and contradictory.

What's more, when on a certain occasion the people wanted to worship Paul and Barnabas, they categorically disallowed it, insisting that they were not gods (Acts 14:14,15). If Jesus were not God, why didn't he take advantage of the occasions in which he was worshiped in order to clarify the misunderstanding? (Matt 14:33; 28:9,17; Luke 24:51,52; John 9:38;

---

7  The expression "making himself equal with God" does not fully reflect the interpretation that the Jews of that day gave to the title "Son of God," an interpretation susceptible to error as some seek to convey. Rather, it is John who, under the inspiration of the Holy Spirit, declares the meaning that "Son of God" has within biblical culture.

16:23,24, etc.) These would have been golden opportunities to openly deny a misunderstood divinity. If the true nature of the Son was not divine but angelic, as some people claim, when people tried to worship him it would have been proper for him to have said, just as angels said in identical situations: "Do not do it! I am a fellow servant with you ... Worship God!" (Rev 19:10; 22:8,9).

But Jesus (the Son) was never against anyone worshiping him. Even the angels had to worship him (Heb 1:6). Why did he not prevent them from worshiping him, thus denying being God? Because both the apostles and the angels, just as he himself did, knew beyond a shadow of a doubt that the Son is God!

## Jesus Talks with God

When Jesus spoke of God the Father, or dialogued with him, was he referring to a different being, or rather, as defined in the Trinity, was he talking with another person within the Divinity? The Scriptures clearly explain it:

- The Son is God; the Father and the Son are the same God (see Chapter 4, sections a–d).

- The Son speaks with the Father in terms of "I" and "you," and the Father speaks the same way regarding the Son. So, two different personalities are detected, dialoguing with each other.

To accept both of these premises, just as the Holy Scriptures present them, is to accept an essential definition of the doctrine of the Trinity. There is nothing strange about the Father and the Son appearing as distinct persons. It is what we have been saying from the beginning: that they are distinct persons but the same God.

We find this duality not only in the New Testament (Injil) but also in the Old Testament (Taurat, Zabur):

> "The Lord said to my Lord" (Ps 110:1 with Matt 22:44; Mark 12:36; Luke 20:42,43; Acts 2:34,35; 1 Cor 15:25; Eph 1:20–22; Col 3:1; Heb 1:13; 8:1; 10:12,13). The Lord God speaks with the Lord God.

> "Your throne, O God ... Therefore God, your God, has anointed you" (Ps 45:6,7 ESV; cf. Heb 1:8,9). God anoints God.

*"And the LORD said to Satan, "The LORD rebuke you, O Satan! The LORD who has chosen Jerusalem rebuke you" (Zech 3:2)!*

The LORD (Yahweh), speaking in first person, says that the LORD (Yahweh), speaking to yet a third person, rebukes Satan.

These are only a few examples showing passages in which God is clearly depicted as an "I" speaking to God himself as a "you."

Diagram of the dialogue between the Father and the Son:

It is not a dialogue between two distinct beings and their respective persons (2), but between two consciences (persons) that coexist in the same being (1).

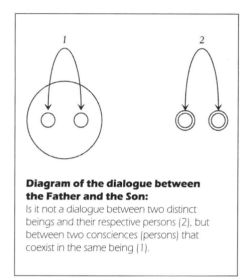

**Diagram of the dialogue between the Father and the Son:**
Is it not a dialogue between two distinct beings and their respective persons (2), but between two consciences (persons) that coexist in the same being (1).

Figure 8

What is more, when the Son entered the space-time sphere of the universe, "emptying himself of his glory," with even more reason, from this new human perspective, he spoke to God in second person. And although "the eternal Son" is in essence greater than the angels (not to mention that he is greater than humans, see Heb 1:2–4), by humbling himself to the condition of a slave (Phil 2:6,7), he referred to the Father (John 14:28), even the angels (Heb 2:9), and even humans (Ps 22:6) as being greater than he as regards to the glory received.

*"If you loved me, you would have rejoiced, because I am going to the Father, for the Father is greater than I" (John 14:28 ESV).*

*"But we see Jesus, who was made a little lower than the angels" (Heb 2:9).*

*"But I am a worm and not a man ... Those who passed by hurled insults at him, shaking their heads ... They said ... 'He trusts in God. Let God rescue him now if he wants him'" (Ps 22:6 with Matt 27:39,43; Mark 15:29; Luke 23:35).*

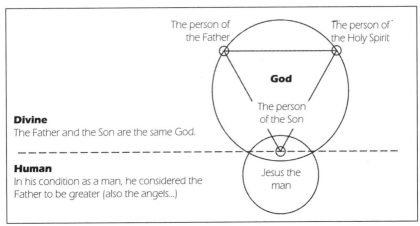

Figure 9

In the texts quoted above, in which Christ compares himself with God, angels, or man, there is no explicit reference to his divinity, but his condition of humility is clearly implied. It can be alleged that this is a personal and subjective interpretation. But even if it is personal and subjective, it is an inescapable conclusion based on the complete absence of biblical declarations directly or indirectly denying the divinity of the Son, whereas there are unmistakable declarations that do affirm his divinity.

In John 14:28, Jesus is not comparing the nature of Jesus with the nature of God, since other passages categorically affirm that he *is* God. Neither does Hebrews 2:9 compare his spiritual nature to that of angels, since he is infinitely superior to them. Neither of course is it compared in Psalm 22:6 to human nature because it would thereby affirm that he is, at least, equal to any man, and even greater than any man because he had no sin. The reference in all three cases is that made to the attitude of the one who lowered himself below everything and everyone.

At the same time, we must not think about Jesus as being solely God; his human condition is equally important. And while he was on earth, he spoke to the Father as any other person did! The following diagram shows the delicate balance between Jesus being Son of God in personality while at the same time directing himself to God the Father as a human being.

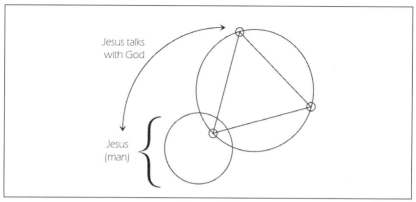

Figure 10

## The Son Is Yahweh Himself

Is the Son a different God from Yahweh (the only and absolute God), as some heretical explanations claim? Is not the Son the same God as the Father? If it were not this way, we would be worshiping two gods. *Hasha!*[8] The Bible once again answers categorically: "To us a son is given ... and he will be called ... Mighty God, Everlasting Father" (Isa 9:6); "A voice cries: 'In the wilderness prepare the way of the LORD [Yahweh]; make straight in the desert a highway for our God ... Behold your God! Behold, the Lord GOD comes with might ... He will tend his flock like a shepherd" (Isa 40:3,4,9,11); "I will raise up for David a righteous Branch—a symbol of Christ—and he shall reign as king ... he will be called: 'The LORD [Yahweh] is our righteousness'" (Jer 23:5,6). See also Chapters 3 and 4 of this book.

An objection, however, that is made to these clear statements from the Scriptures is: "If this is true, how come Jesus does not know the date on which he will return to earth and his Father does?" (see Mark 13:32). If Jesus is truly the same God as the Father, how come he does not know these things? As we saw in Philippians 2:6, the Son, during the time of his humiliation, relinquished his magnificence. That is, he made the decision to not take advantage of his divine attributes. Even though he shares the divine essence—in his being and person, he identified with

---

8    *"Hasha"* is a religious expression in Islam that is repeated so as to deny any sinful declaration or statement about God.

and appropriated human nature[9]—taking on the form of a servant—and limited himself to the conditions of earthly life. That is, as a man he delegated his knowledge, power, and decisions to the initiative of the Father; he limited himself not to know or say anything of his own accord (see Matt 26:39; John 5:19,30; 6:38; 8:28; 12:49; 14:10).

Knowledge is not a fundamental element of the being or of the personality; that is, someone is not a person because of what they know but because of their constitution. Let's consider an example: if Ali suffers a memory loss due to a blow on the head, the fact that he does not remember everything does not change his nature or constitution, nor does it strip him of his human personality. He is not someone different, even when he suffers a memory lapse. Jesus set aside his attributes, but he did not become stripped from his being or from his divine personality. He voluntarily suffered a "memory loss"—here, of course, we are speaking figuratively—in matters such as the one we are discussing. But, as a result of that, he is not a person different from God, nor is his divinity altered. Since this figurative "amnesia" was voluntary, he could regain "his memory" or benefit from divine knowledge at any moment he wished.

It is quite clear that "omniscience" is an attribute intrinsic to divinity. But in the case of Christ, God, in his sovereignty and omnipotence, can alter even that without committing an outrage against his divine integrity. It was not God the Son, but Jesus the man,[10] who did not know the date of his return to earth.

The important thing in Mark 13:32 is the way in which the Son identifies so closely with us, human beings. How could the Son (the *Kalimat'ullahi*) strip himself of his knowledge when he took on the form of human nature? Undoubtedly, any attempt to resolve this question, apart from the biblical explanation that he "made himself nothing, taking the very nature of a servant" (Phil 2:7), falls short, and our explanations and illustrations are insufficient. The fact that our finite minds cannot completely understand it simply proves that God is infinite. We cannot subordinate the evidence of revelation to the logic of reason. Revelation

---

9   In theology, "nature" is called the communication of the attributes.

10  As we will see right away, Christ's humanity was not a mere corporal wrapping but also included a human personality (spirit and soul) that participated fully in all the characteristics belonging to man's nature (with the exception of sin), including his limitations.

has its logic, for it expresses a reality, and reality is always coherent. But its logic is above human logic. And thankfully it is that way! Otherwise, God would be less intelligent than his creatures. He is capable of carrying out what in our minds is inconceivable!

To appeal to the superiority of logic and divine coherence is not a way to escape from an unsolvable dilemma. The question is not whether we can understand the exhaustive form of Christ's divinity and humanity. The truth is that God has revealed it, and therefore it is a fact! If we cannot resolve it by logic, we can understand it intuitively in a spiritual way.

Another question is how can the only God be in the body of Jesus and at the same time be omnipresent? Air fills the entire atmosphere. If I cover the mouth of a glass with my hand, air continues to be both inside and outside of the glass. In the same way, God fills the entire universe and overflows it, as he is not bound by either time or space. The God that is "inside" Jesus and the God that is "outside" is the same. However, only the person of the Son resides specifically in Jesus.

By way of conclusion: the Logos manifested in Jesus is the very same God and Yahweh himself!

## The God-Man

How then must we understand the fact of the "incarnation"? There are two different natures in Jesus Christ—one human and the other divine—that participate in a single "self." In the Council of Chalcedon the issue was rightly defined: Jesus is not a deified man—he is God who has become human without losing his divinity (see John 1:14). Therefore, two natures coexist in him in a single person. This is called a "hypostatic union." This union is not the synthesis, fusion, or mixture of two natures but rather the combination of two integral natures that coincide in a single person.

Just as the diagram shows, Jesus, in his condition as man, does not take on the role of sovereign but of servant, a servant whose personality is divine— the Son. Once again, as man—that is, his strictly human nature—he does not access divine knowledge but rather participates in the personality of the Son. Likewise, he is not omnipresent but rather is limited to time and space. He is a man! However, as God he has neither lost his omnipotence, nor his omniscience, nor his omnipresence. These are not attributes of human nature but of the person of the Son. As a person—the Son, he participates equally in the divine and human natures. We can imagine this as two telephones connected to a single switchboard. One of the telephones is open to international calls and the other one is not. But the switchboard that the two telephones share connects them to a single network. The switchboard would be the person of the Son and, through this person, even the local telephone can make international calls.

The divinity of Jesus does not mix with his humanity, and much less with his body! Even his mind and soul are human; they are not of divine "substance." But his "self" participates in both his divinity and humanity.

Figure 11

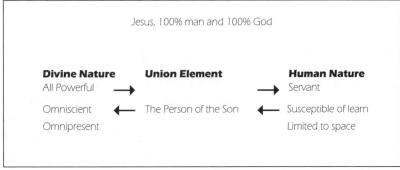

Figure 12

Consider the light given off by a lightbulb. The lightbulb is not the electricity, nor is the electricity the lightbulb, but both of them operate to give light. The electric current passes through the lightbulb, and this same electricity turns on the filament and shines as light. The lightbulb and the electricity participate in giving the same light and are joined together by it. But neither is the lightbulb electricity, nor does the electricity reduce itself to a lightbulb!

The divine substance (*wujud*) did not become a body in Jesus Christ. That is, the flesh of Jesus was not God. God was not transformed into a man by abandoning his divine condition; the divine "substance" was not transformed into human nature. What became a body was the divine identity—*dhat* of the Son. And this is the person that participates in the divine nature. Of course, we are before an unexplainable mystery!

This union is an exclusive prerogative of Jesus:

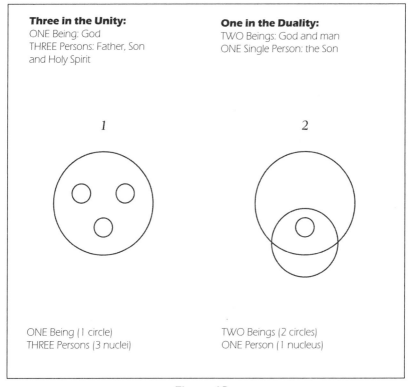

**Three in the Unity:**
ONE Being: God
THREE Persons: Father, Son
and Holy Spirit

**One in the Duality:**
TWO Beings: God and man
ONE Single Person: the Son

1

2

ONE Being (1 circle)
THREE Persons (3 nuclei)

TWO Beings (2 circles)
ONE Person (1 nucleus)

Figure 13

*It does not look like the union that exists within the Trinity.* Whereas in the Trinity three persons exist in a single substance or divine essence, in Jesus Christ there is one single person in two substances; a single "self" that gathers them together. That is, the Trinity is more like the illustration of the electricity, where a single element is manifest in *three* different states (power, light, heat). On the other hand, the union of the two natures in Christ is more like the lightbulb, where *one* single state—the light—participates in two distinct elements: the electric current and the lightbulb. In one case there is a single element and three manifestations of energy. In the other there are two elements and one specific manifestation of energy. In the Trinity there is one nature and three persons; in Christ there are two natures and one person.

*It is not an organic union (that is, the mixing of the two natures), but rather it is verified in the realm of the "self."* The result of boiling tea leaves in water is the mixture of the two. We therefore no longer perceive the tea and the water separately. This is a mixture, an infusion. The case of Jesus is completely opposite, because he is not half God and half man; nor do his humanity and divinity combine in him. It is not an organic union.

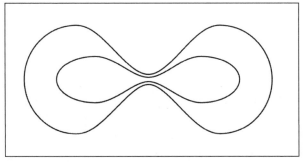

Figure 14

*Neither is it the same as the union of the Holy Spirit with the believer.* This is a union where there is a "host" and a "guest." It is the union of two separate and distinct persons, the believer and the Holy Spirit; and of two distinct natures, a human being and God, perfectly differentiated one from the other. This situation of the believer and the Holy Spirit is more similar to—if I can use the expression—that of the prophet Jonah in the belly of the whale. Both the mind of Jonah and that of the whale were distinct, and their bodies were also different at the same time. The union that exists in Jesus is not reduced to the indwelling of the Spirit of God in a man.

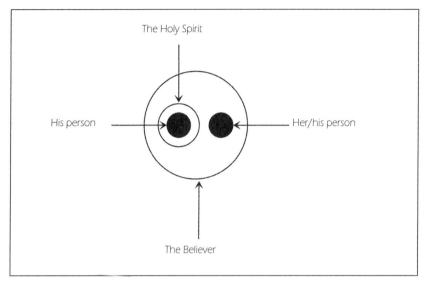

Figure 15

The divine nature did not suffer any alteration in the incarnation. What became human was not divine substance but the person of the Son. We are therefore not talking about God becoming incarnated and losing his divinity, nor are we talking about a man named Jesus attaining divinity. We must understand the humanity and body of Christ as a temple in which God is present. The expression used in John 1:14, "And the Word became flesh and *dwelt* among us" (emphasis added) means exactly "the Word became flesh and pitched his tent (he tabernacled) among us." In this expression, the body of Christ is compared to the tabernacle in the times of Moses. Along this same line, John 2:21 says, "But he was speaking about the temple of his body." That is, from the perspective of his humanity, we can think of Jesus as a tabernacle; and from the perspective of his divinity, as the one who inhabits or dwells in the tabernacle.

Every time that Jesus makes reference to himself he speaks of a single "person." Everything that Jesus said and did, it was said and done by a single "self," whether through his human condition or his divine condition, or both at the same time.

The acts of Jesus, such as creating the universe or preserving it, come from his eternal and omnipresent divine "self" (the Word is in Jesus and also fills the entire universe while also transcending it). Creation was not a prerogative of his humanity, because the man Jesus did not exist in the act of creation; only the Son of God—the eternal Word—existed.

Eating, sleeping, resting, etc., are acts of the "self," however, they are not needs of the Son but needs of his human condition.

His supernatural actions, such as miracles, emanate from the "self" by the combined action of two natures. The real cause is the divine Person; his humanity is the instrument, through his mind, faith, and will.

When Jesus died on the cross, his body and his humanity died[11] but not his divinity—in the same way that when a lightbulb breaks it doesn't occur to us to say that the light has broken or that the electricity has been cut off. Nonetheless, since his human "self" is the same "self" of the Logos, the value of his expiation is infinite, as is infinite the Son of God.

The divine Word, by its own definition, is God from eternity to eternity. On the other hand, Jesus Christ, as man, appears at a specific moment in the course of history. Said differently, it is impossible for the Son to not be God. And in the same way the Son was not forced to take on the human condition.

When we refer with our words to the "self" of the Son of God, we can attribute any situation or action to either his humanity or divinity without distinguishing between the two natures. Continuing with the examples given, it is like seeing the president, king, or ruler of our country on television, we point at the screen and exclaim, "Look, our leader!" Although we are pointing at both the image and at the screen, we do not confuse the two things. Likewise, when we say, "Mom, Dad's on the phone. He wants to talk with you," we do not confuse our father with the telephone. Following the same rationale we can say, "the Son of God died on the cross," "God became man," or "this man is God." Jesus, as man, can be the object of our prayers and of our worship. Because in reality we are referring to his "self," and his "self" is God!

---

11  In fact, death is not the annihilation of the self (being), but the separation of the corporeal entity from the spiritual entity. When we say that his humanity dies that does not mean that he ceased to be man, rather—as in the death of any person—his soul became disassociated from his body until the moment of the resurrection.

# 7

# CLUES TO UNDERSTANDING THE TRINITY

At risk of oversimplifying the subject, we are going to take advantage first of some basic philosophical concepts in order to understand better the ontological necessity for the existence of the Trinity.[1]

One of philosophy's fundamental intentions is to answer the question: How do we know and how can we know that we know? This branch of philosophy is known as "epistemology," which is the doctrine of the nature and methods of scientific knowledge. In order to reach an answer, one must first define existence or being.

Philosophical posits for explaining the existence of the universe are innumerable. All of them, however, agree on one issue: there is "something" in the universe and we cannot say "nothing exists." But, how did this "something" come into existence? The ability to formulate a coherent answer to this question is what will keep any philosophical posit standing or send it tumbling down without any credibility whatsoever.

The second question to consider is, how did conscience or personality originate in the universe? We can reduce life to a set of physiochemical cause-and-effect principles and reactions, but even so the difference between a human being and a machine is unexplainably greater than mere structural or functional alterations. We cannot reduce conscience to laboratory formulas!

---

1    The ontological argument for the existence of God attempts the method of a priori proof, which uses intuition and reason alone. In the context of the Abrahamic religions, ontological arguments were first proposed by the medieval philosopher Avicenna in *The Book of Healing*, cited in: Steve A. Johnson, "Ibn Sina's Fourth Ontological Argument for God's Existence," *The Muslim World* 74 (1984): iii–iv, 161–71.

The Trinity is not only the best answer to these questions but is also the only coherent answer.

There are only four possible explanations to the origin of the universe:

1. There was previously a state in which nothing existed and now something exists.

2. Everything started with "something" impersonal (matter, energy).

3. Everything started with a conscious and personal being.

4. A "dual principle" has always existed (dualism).

No one has ever opted for the first explanation. Neither has anyone ever presented the fourth option clearly. The impersonal principle is the most widely held view in the secular West and is also the one being exported to other cultures. In fact, in a different way, it is also the foundation of the Far Eastern cosmology. But this opinion cannot explain the existence of the world, nor is it compatible with the order of the cosmos—due to the law of entropy everything in the universe tends to disorder. Even more relevant is the fact that an impersonal origin of the universe will never be able to provide a satisfactory explanation for the origin of conscience and personality.

The option presented in the Bible indicates that conscience and personality existed from before the universe. So, conscience, love, and personality constituted—and still constitute—the eternal "nucleus" of the Being who has given existence to everything.

## Eternal Love Makes the Trinity an Imperative

The greatest manifestation of this conscience and personality cannot be other than love. "God is love" (1 John 4:8,16). The essence of love is giving oneself for "another"; to love entails loving someone; love needs a lover and a loved one. If God, in his unique self, did not exist as a plural personality from eternity past, he would have not been able to share his love with anyone. He would have been subject to creating angels and human beings (or similar beings) in order to share his love, and would have depended on his creation for developing his affinities. Nevertheless, God created the world as an act of complete freedom of his will, not out of necessity, since the torrent of his love has flowed perfectly between the

Father and the Son, and through the Holy Spirit, since time immemorial. Thus the Son, the Second Person of the Trinity, says to the Father: "because you loved me before the creation of the world" (John 17:24).

Some Islamic thinkers maintain that "God's attributes, as manifestations of his essential being, have a temporal beginning and therefore result from the fiat (*kun:* كُنْ) of Allah, who gives them names at the moment of their creation." It is for this reason that they reject that God is love: "because love is the action of someone who loves, not the person who loves. In the same way knowledge or the word are actions of the conscience and not of the person's essence."[2] This is a logical reasoning, but it obviates the truths revealed in the Bible. We, as people of the Book (*ahlu'l-Kitab:* أهل الكتاب), when it comes to examining and defining God's exact nature and personality, depend, first of all, not only on human reason but on divine revelation; which is not at all illogical. When we humbly accept revealed truth as such, it is not difficult to later discover its intrinsic logic and coherence.

He is immutable (unchanging, without variation) in his being and attributes, and one of them is his condition of Creator God. So, was or was he not Creator before bringing about the universe's existence? He was, because in eternity past he was the generating cause of the Word and the Spirit. What does the Logos say about himself and of his eternal existence in the heart of the Divinity? "The LORD brought me forth as the first of his works, before his deeds of old; I was appointed from eternity" (Prov 8:22,23). God is Creator because he "created"[3] from eternity and he is always "creating."[4] In the same manner, God has always spoken, as he in fact did in a particular and personal way from eternity, because, from before the beginning, the Word was with God and at the same time was God.

---

2  Abdulahad Davud, "Mahoma: Según el Antiguo y Nuevo Testamento," in *Muhammad in the Bible* (Al-Kitab Publications, 1991), 13.

3  Here we should say "generated" because the flow of the Word and of the Spirit from the divine essence, even though it encompasses tremendous creativity it is not an act of space-time creation.

4  In Islam, the general idea is that each change, movement, even life itself, is an uninterrupted and direct, creative act of God. This concept is closely related to that of a fatalistic predestination in which a person's destiny and decisions are a submissive reflection of divine decrees. Of course, when we say here that he "is always creating" we are referring to the fact that he sustains the universe, infuses it with life, and administrates it through his providence, but we are not referring to a mechanistic control that would reduce every free will to a mere puppet show.

This intrinsic creativity or communicability of the Divinity is not the act of creating elements that are distinct from his being. Neither does he create his own attributes in a temporal sequence. His eternal attributes are atemporal expressions in the same way that the three divine Persons that form his substantial being are atemporal. As a result the Holy Scriptures use the Hebrew word "to possess" (*qanah:* קָנָה) and not "to create" (*bara:* בָּרָא) in the passage quoted from Proverbs. Therefore, his attributes are not created (*makhluq:* مخلوق), nor of a later existence (*hadith:* حديث); they simply have no beginning (*qadim:* قديم). His attributes do not become confused with his own being, but neither are they different from or independent of him. All of them converge in his living Word and in his Holy Spirit, who from eternity past are distinguished as well-defined persons within the Divinity.

## The Incommensurable God

God exists outside of the confines of time and space and beyond any possibility of change. As a result he can exist in three persons, even though we are unable to comprehend it. At every instant he knows the past, the present, and the future. We can even say that he is in the past, present, and future at the same time: "With the Lord a day is like a thousand years, and a thousand years are like a day" (2 Pet 3:8).

God can exist in three different persons at the same time, just as he can be present everywhere at the same time. "You hem me in, behind and before, and lay your hand upon me. Such knowledge is too wonderful for me; it is high; I cannot attain it. Where shall I go from your Spirit? Or where shall I flee from your presence? If I ascend to heaven, you are there! If I make my bed in Sheol, you are there" (Ps 139:5–8 ESV)!

God can be here and one thousand kilometers away simultaneously. The presence of God here is not a part of him but is God in his fullness. And at the same time his presence one thousand kilometers away is not a part of him but the very same God in all his fullness. We therefore have God in two different places but not two gods. How is this possible? It is possible because he is in eternity (outside of time), where there are no spatial limitations.

To say that God has no beginning is confusing to us from the point of view of human logic. But this fact is an immovable pillar in every monotheistic faith. It is also a principle he himself has revealed: God is eternal.

*"I was appointed from eternity, from the beginning, before the world began ... I was there" (Prov 8:23,27).*

God knows all things:

*"You know when I sit and when I rise; you perceive my thoughts from afar ... Before a word is on my tongue you know it completely, O LORD" (Ps 139:2,4).*

He can tend to millions of people talking to him at once in prayer. How is this possible? As humans, if two people talk to us at once we are unable to make heads or tails of the conversation; imagine if a million people were talking to us! And yet, the one who exists in eternity can set aside personal and individual "time" for each speaker!

In and of himself God is a mystery for us. If he were not and we were able to perceive him perfectly, he would not be God because he would fit into our finite mind. We cannot understand him fully, but we can discover what he has revealed about himself, and we can understand the need and the logic of these spiritual truths.

## Let's Recapitulate

In the Divinity three persons are "unfolded." These three personal states, eternal and continuous, are as if a single mass of water could at the same time be vapor, liquid, and solid. In the physical realm this is only possible in sequences: first vapor through boiling, then water by condensation, and finally ice through freezing. But it is impossible to have these three states at the same time in the same mass of water.

We are unable to conceive of God in a sequence, within the limits of space and time. The differentiation between the three persons of the Trinity occurs outside of time. The person of the Father, when expressing the Word, is manifested as source and origin. The living Word, emanating from the Father and pronounced by the Father from eternity past, is manifested in turn as a different identity. And the life principle between the Father and the Son, which is love, is manifested in the breath of the Spirit in the heart of the Divinity. But in all of this, there is neither a "before" nor an "after."

God's proper name is Yahweh. All the other names that have been given to him: Elohim (Hebrew), Zeus (Greek), Allah (Arabic), Tanri

(Turkish), God (English), Dios (Spanish), etc., are nothing more than the generic name used to identify and distinguish the supreme Being. Even the majority of these names are qualifiers used formerly to refer to the dominant god in the polytheistic pantheon of other beliefs; including the name Allah, in its pre-Islamic use.[5] On the other hand, Yahweh is the only name that does not come from any human culture but has been revealed directly by God (Ex 3:1–6). It is his original and authentic name. What does it mean? It signifies "I AM WHO I AM." It is the definition of his very own existence (Ex 3:14).

We find an "I" and a "he" that are a single being. Additionally, the verbal conjugation expresses a continuous present. That is, this "I" and this "he" do not have a "before" nor an "after" but an uninterrupted "now."

We must remember that, at the same time that God is himself, he is also the Logos—*Kalam*—that exists at the very heart of the Divinity. The Bible defines this Logos as the Word or divine Wisdom. This Word has his own personality in the heart of the Divinity and is as perfect as God because he is the very same God. And the current of love, which is also conscious and flows through them both, is the Holy Spirit, as we have already mentioned.

Each divine Person defines his identity in relation and in contrast to the other two persons. In God there is an "I," a "you," and a "he." For this reason God can say to God, "I love you." Just as we see in these verses: "The LORD says to my Lord" (Ps 110:1); "Therefore God, your God, has anointed you" (Ps 45:6,7); or "And the LORD said ... 'The LORD rebuke you'" (Zech 3:2 ESV).

Jesus speaks to the Father as a second person for two reasons:

1. Jesus is the Second Person of the Trinity (the Son).

2. After taking on human nature he also spoke to the Father as a man.

---

5    Cyril Glassé, *The New Encyclopedia of Islam: A Revised Edition of the Concise Encyclopedia of Islam*, s.v. "Allah."

## Fullness and Self-submission within God

Now we will try to give an approximate explanation as to how three persons in the Divinity are mutually and uninterruptedly generated in eternity. As we have already seen, this fact does not have either a "before" nor an "after," so it is therefore not a "creation" but a continuous "generation."

The Father pronounces the Word. This living "expression" is fulfilled in the fullness of the Father. In one sense the Father pours his self into the Son. And the Father and the Son pour their self into the Spirit. What does this really mean?

According to the theory of relativity, time does not exist at the speed of light. Using this concept of quantum physics we have an illustration of how the three persons of the Trinity can participate of a single substance. But we must not forget that with such illustrations we are not comparing nor reducing the Divinity to the examples. The true purpose of any illustration is to show the viability and the logic of a spiritual reality. Invisible realities can be understood better thanks to visible examples that help us to visualize them.

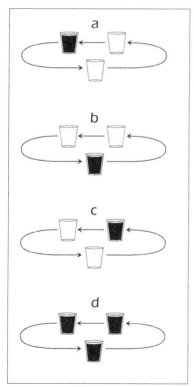

Figure 16

Let's imagine three teacups, one of them is full, the other two are empty (Figure 16a). We pour the tea from the first cup into the second (Figure 16b) and then pour this one into the third (Figure 16c). Then we pour the tea in the third cup back into the first one. The cups are thus being filled consecutively with the tea from one cup. Now let's imagine that we accelerate the process. As speed increases in the transfer, the eye is less able to distinguish the separate movements, until the point arrives in which the three cups seem to be full at the same time (Figure 16d).

If we were able to reach the speed of light in this succession of emptying and filling, the three cups would truly be filled with one single cup of tea! That is, instead of one full cup and two empty cups we would have three cups full of the tea from one of the cups! The filling and emptying succession would be occurring outside of the realm of time, in what would be a constant or continuous "now."

Something like this occurs in the Trinity. The constant flow and filling of the Divinity perpetuates in eternity (the absence of time). So God the Father pours his self into the Son and generates the way he exists. And in the same fashion both of them generate the way that the Spirit exists. Father, Son, and Holy Spirit are full "at the same time" with a single being (the substance of the only God). And at the same time they subsist in three personal "molds," that is, as three different personalities; like three different cups filled at the same time with the tea from only one cup. The same and single Being who fills the Divinity, at the same time adopts the different identities of Father, Son, and Holy Spirit; just as the tea adopts the shape of the different cups that it fills. If we can imagine this scene, which occurs beyond the threshold of time, suddenly the Trinity becomes a tremendously logical and simple reality.

When a three-bladed propeller is stopped we can see the three blades perfectly. But when it spins at full speed we see the image of a perfect disc; it seems as if the three blades are at all points of the circle at the same time. In some instances we even see on one side the disc shape made by the propeller and on the other side the shadow of the three blades turning slowly inside the circle, even in the opposite direction. In reality each of these shadows is made by the intersection of the three blades at the same time. Of course, this is nothing more than a visual illusion, but if this turning were to occur beyond the limitations of time the three blades would simultaneously be at different points from each other and at the very same point of the circle. This is somewhat like what scientists state regarding the electron that revolves at the speed of light, and so it cannot be stated that it is located at any single point in its orbit around the nucleus of the atom.

In this way the three persons of the Trinity also manifest themselves as the one and only God. They are not three parts of the Divinity; the three of them possess "separately" the fullness of the same Deity. But they are not three gods. They are like the three cups filled from the tea of a single cup. It is as if each person of the Trinity is continuously bursting forth from the others while at the same time being at the climax of his fullness, since this bursting forth and fullness occurs outside of time.

Each person, by emanating from the other two, owes his life to the absolute emptying into himself of the other two. This emptying does not consist in ceasing to be or to exist but in giving oneself in favor of the other, renouncing oneself and renouncing one's own "rights." We see this in the humiliation of the Son who "emptied Himself, taking the form of a bond-servant" (Phil 2:7 NASB). Although his attitude of being a servant is associated with his humanity, it is in fact prior to his incarnation; it is an eternal disposition of the Son towards the Father. But this emptying also expresses the manner in which the three persons of the Trinity fill each other.

Due to each person emptying himself into the others, each of them is "inside" the other, and for that reason the three are a single being: "the Father is in me and I am in the Father"; "Do you not believe that I am in the Father and the Father is in me? ... the Father who dwells in me does his works"; "Believe Me that I am in the Father and the Father is in Me"; "you, Father, are in me, and I in you" (see John 10:38; 14:10,11; 17:21).

The conclusion of all this is that the life principle or motor of each person of the Trinity is not to reserve his fullness for himself but to totally give himself on behalf of the others; that is, absolute love!

For this reason true love is always expressed in the form of submission: "For God so loved the world, that he gave his only begotten Son" (John 3:16); "the Son of God, who loved me and gave himself for me" (Gal 2:20); "as Christ loved us and gave himself up for us" (Eph 5:2); "as Christ loved the church and gave himself up for her" (Eph 5:25).

In the same way, the circle of love in the Divinity becomes ever tighter in a process of successive and total submission God is love because his very essence is love. The demonstration of his love in the vicarious sacrifice of Jesus Christ for our sins is nothing but a faint sparkle in contrast to the original and essential love that shines in the bosom of the Divinity itself. And it is for this reason that the Father glorifies the Son, the Son glorifies the Father, and the Holy Spirit glorifies the Son and the Father.

*"Jesus answered, 'If I glorify myself, my glory is nothing. It is my Father who glorifies me'" (John 8:54 ESV).*

*"Father, glorify your name" (John 12:28).*

*"Now is the Son of Man glorified, and God is glorified in him. If God is glorified in him, God will also glorify him in himself" (John 13:31,32 ESV).*

*"... that the Father may be glorified in the Son" (John 14:13 ESV).*

*"When the Spirit of truth comes ... he will not speak on his own authority, but whatever he hears he will speak ... He will glorify me, for he will take what is mine and declare it to you. All that the Father has is mine" (John 16:13–15 ESV).*

*"Father ... glorify your Son that the Son may glorify you" (John 17:1 ESV).*

*"I glorified you on earth ... And now, Father, glorify me in your own presence with the glory that I had with you before the world existed" (John 17:4,5 ESV).*

In this way the Father gives all that he is to the Son, because when he "generates" him, he transfers the totality of his eternal self (except his condition of Father). And in the same way the Father and the Son "breathe into" and "send," respectively, the Spirit.

In John 1:1, the expression that translates as "was with God" (*pros ton Zeon*) literally means "was in the direction of God." That is, the Son also emptied himself into the Father. This is not a "generation" (the Father does not come from the Son), because what returns from the Word—*Kalam*—to the Father is the echo of the Word. That is, the Father expresses the Son—the Word— with divine perfection, and the Son defines with divine perfection what the Father is, reflecting the Father like a mirror. The eternal Word defines the Divinity to perfection, completely, to the point of containing the divine substance and perfection. And this uninterrupted transfer takes place at the very heart of the only God, in the continuous "now" of eternity.

When I see my face in the mirror, it is my face that produces the reflection. My reflection describes me and returns to me in the form of an image. But this image does not determine what I am like, nor does it shape me. The reflection or echo of the Word is a voluntary submission, but it is not a state of inferiority. This voluntary submission increases—if it can be said this way—with the incarnation because, in the person of the Son, the incarnate Word is also subjected as man to God and, being in this state, considers God greater than himself.

The Word that emanates from the heart of the Father at the same time remains in the Father. A person generates an idea, puts it into words, and then pronounces them. The words come out of his or her mouth, and after resonating they dissipate and "die." It is not at all like this in the Divinity. The Son is not the same as the words of God but rather *is* the Word of God. That is, the Son is the originating expression—the *kalam nafsi*—that gives shape to all of God's words, and does not change nor die. He is somewhat like a person's vocabulary, forming phrases and pouring them into words, but in doing so, instead of becoming depleted, the vocabulary becomes enriched.

For a human it is not possible to give oneself to another without losing something, without emptying oneself. When a believer, however, becomes a partaker of the divine love (Rom 5:5; 2 Pet 1:4) he or she reaches true fullness when they give themselves for others. They can finally sacrifice themselves without being consumed, without losing anything and without emptying themselves.

This giving of oneself is comparable to the relationship between past, present, and future. The instant just lived becomes the past as time moves forward. The present earns its existence as time flows from the future to the past, in a continuous transformation from one stage to the other. The future transforms unceasingly into the present, which in turn transforms nonstop into the past. Every instant is therefore participant in a before, a now, and an after. The before and after are the extremes, the vertices of the instant; the now is the nucleus. And in this uninterrupted flow of the cosmic clock, the three dimensions of time never mix with each other, nor is their order inverted, rather they exist within their own autonomous stages. The three cover the totality of time; all instants are, have been, or will be; present, past, and future. Separately, the three constitute the three basic facets of time. And yet they are all—in reality—one and the same instant!

The same thing can be said about movement, time, and space—concepts that define the structure of the universe and that mutually complement each other. The existence of each one of them is dependent on the other two. Time—our concept of it—is the division of the change or movement registered within a given space and expressed in portions of unit. If there were no movement or space there would be no time; without time or space there would be no movement, in the same way that without movement or time neither would there be space. The three exist as an inseparable whole.

The entire universe, as the masterpiece of the triune God, is made up of the combination of triads of complementary elements:

- energy, material, and speed
- gas, liquid, and solid
- width, depth, and height
- body, soul, and spirit
- thought, expression, and action
- power, light, and heat
- thesis, antithesis, and synthesis
- before, now, and after
- mind, feelings, and will

Of course, all of these are nothing more than reflections or shadows of the Creator's designs. In a certain measure, however, they reflect his glory and his triune condition, although they do not describe it.

## The Triune Condition and Its Mystery

Truth is always reasonable. But not all that seems logical to us is necessarily true. Revelation is true. And if we do not understand it when we first approach it, that does not mean we ought to reject it. Whoever seeks, finds; and whoever wants to understand, will.

As considered previously, among the essential characteristics of the Divinity is the fact that God is love. His condition of absolute God, infinite, self-sufficient, and loving, demands the presence of an active and a passive, of a sender and a receiver within the God-self, opposing poles that we have been calling divine Persons.

Group relations need a minimum (and a maximum) of three persons to be perfect and complete.[6] In geometry the most elementary shape of a surface is the triangle. No geometric figure exists with only two sides, and a polygon with four sides or more is not an expression of the simplest figure. So the most perfect and elemental representation of a surface or area is the triangle. Quite possibly this is why the figure that best helps us to express the Trinity schematically is the triangle.

The triangle is the minimum expression enabling us to enclose a flat surface within a defined area. A single line can cross a space, but it does not define a plane, nor does it enclose a surface. Two lines that intersect do not configure a defined geometric figure (although they do define an infinite plane). But three nonparallel lines that intersect with each other perfectly delimit a concrete area. The sides of a triangle connect the vertices at the same time that they separate them. Likewise, the three sides participate in a single surface.

In a similar way, in the divine center there is an "I," a "you," and a "he." They are distinguished from each other by their relationships, but they participate of a single and same divine substance. And the most perfect form of this relationship is the triad in the unit (*tathlith fee'l-tauhid:* تثليث في التوحيد).

We are not saying here that the Trinity is truth because we have elaborated a logical explanation; rather, we are saying that we can find a logical explanation—whether it satisfies us or not—which helps us to understand it, because the Trinity is a spiritual reality. And the reality is coherent.

When Jesus, speaking of the Holy Spirit, says that "whatever he hears he will speak" (John 16:13), the Holy Spirit is defined as a third person that hears the eternal dialogue between the Father and the Son. Here we see a group relationship: a "he" hears and communicates what an "I" and a "you" in the group are speaking. If God himself had not revealed the Trinity in the Scriptures, no one would have ever dared to formulate such a doctrine (among other reasons because no one would be capable

---

6   Why three and not four or five? Apart from the fact that the Bible reveals that there are three—which is the only and true proof that it is so—once again reason helps us understand the need for there to be three. It is logical to think that God experiences group relationships without having to depend on his creatures. That is, "I" and "you" can have a group relationship with a third person, "he." Our relationships not only are with individuals but we also have, at the same time, relationships with groups of individuals.

of imagining or inventing such a fraud). Anyone who examines the biblical text with honesty may choose not to believe its content—no one is forced to believe, but the person will have no choice but to recognize that truly this is the message given to us regarding the nature of God.

God is one. But in his glory, and in a manner that is unfathomable for the human mind, God exists in three persons. This mystery exceeds by far our human intellectual ability because God is outside the bounds of time and space. Humans learn through comparisons and experimenting. And we cannot compare the Trinity to anything else that we know or experience. That is why it is difficult for us to understand it.

A man or a woman is the combination of a single being and a single person. On the other hand, God is three persons in a single being. For that reason we cannot compare him to man nor reduce him to the individuality of a human being. If we insist on maintaining that "He cannot be three persons and must therefore be one person, like ourselves," in reality we are assigning to God the limitations of the creature and falling into the sin of association—shirk.[7] Again, in doing so we are enclosing God within the limits of physics, or within the limits of human conceptual abilities, instead of respectfully accepting what his Word reveals to us. If we say that "He is one, like ourselves" we are then associating him with the structure of creation and the creature itself. Hasha!

What is more natural to God than being supernatural? We cannot understand him exhaustively, but we can know what he has revealed about himself, and we can understand the logic and need for knowing it. The illustrations, although they are not descriptive, do provide us with analogies that unfold for us the logic and viability of the spiritual fact, helping us to understand it.

$$\text{Red light} \cap \text{green light} \cap \text{blue light} = \text{white light}$$

For instance: white light, formed by red, green, and blue rays, once again presents us with a trinity. White light is formed when the three fundamental colors converge. The three colors are light (the same substance),

---

7  Shirk: in Islam, the sin of associating partners with Allah, giving his characteristics to others besides him.

but they are three distinct colors (each having a different quality). And at the same time they form the same light and the same color: white light.

God, in substance, is one God, but in his person he has three identities; the three are the same and only God. This is a mystery, which does not mean that it is illogical. It is simply that, as human beings, limited by time and space, we are unable to comprehend the eternal and are unable to understand all the dimensions of the Trinity. It is in the same way that we cannot see all the sides of a football in a single glance because we ourselves form part of the space that we are observing.

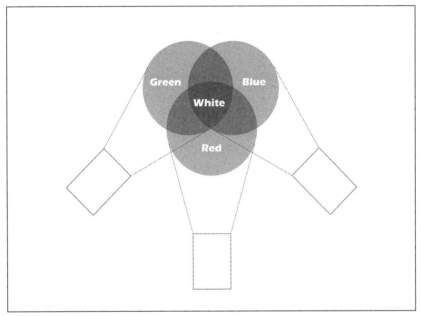

Figure 17

However, it is not only God who remains a mystery to us. Are we able to understand all the mysteries of the universe and answer all the questions that it poses? Well, if we cannot find answers to the enigmas of creation (and the more answers we find the greater the dilemmas that remain unsolved), why should it surprise us if we are not able to solve all the mysteries surrounding God?

According to the theory of relativity, time does not exist at the speed of light. So if two people travel at different speeds, one at a normal speed and the other close to the speed of light, when they meet again they will have aged at different rates. For one, only a few days or months will have passed while for the other it will have been years. Is this really possible? Just as in the case of the Trinity, the explanations are not simple or easy to understand. But the theory of relativity is today the basis for quantum physics and it is completely logical and mathematically correct, even though the majority of us cannot understand it. So then, just because we don't understand something we cannot deny it. This kind of attitude would be like that of the Middle Ages when people refused to accept that the world was round.

Some people, who want to reduce the Trinity to our conceptual framework, affirm that such a doctrine is outside of all logic because 1+1+1=1 is an impossibility. But if we wanted to express this reality as a mathematical formula it would be 1x1x1=1; that is, 1 raised to the power of 3 (the cube of 1), because the existence of God in three persons does not occur either in time or in space. So therefore, instead of units that are added, they are entities that are inside of each other, without occupying space, in the form of 3 in 1. "No one has seen God at any time. The one and only Son, who is in the bosom of the Father, he has declared him" (John 1:18 WEB; see also John 10:38; 14:11; 17:21). As beings that occupy space and time, three humans cannot wear the same shirt at the same time. With great effort they might tear the shirt, each of them ending up with a piece of the shirt and remaining next to each other. On the other hand, the three persons of the Trinity can be imagined as intersecting,

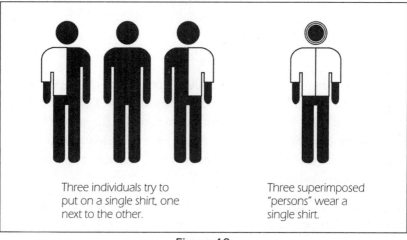

Three individuals try to put on a single shirt, one next to the other.

Three superimposed "persons" wear a single shirt.

Figure 18

one within the others, and wearing a single shirt at the same time. In this case we would have three persons but a single figure wearing the shirt. The persons of the Trinity do not "occupy" the space of three individuals, only of one: three persons in a single individual!

If we force our imagination, we can find many illustrations that will help us to clarify by approximation the logic of the Trinity. What is really important, however, is not to be able to solve the issue in a logical or mathematical way, but to live in a true relationship of commitment to God, according to his attitude towards us as Father, Son, and Holy Spirit; which is what the gospel really seeks.

If there is something that we don't understand, it is difficult to accept. For this reason, at least, it is important that we accept the reality of the Trinity. But once this is resolved, as we have seen in the last section of Chapter 5, what is truly important is to experience salvation, sanctification, a victorious life, a prayer life, and so on, in the fellowship that God has planned for every human being. And this fellowship is with the triune God!

The truth is, it is not so difficult to understand the assumptions of this doctrine. But the essence of this truth is not assimilated only under the effort of a lengthy study of the Bible but in deepening one's relationship with God, because the goal is to know him. In the measure that we pray to God, we follow the example of Christ and we allow the Spirit to act in us; we begin to grow deeper in our devotional life, see how his thoughts and desires take shape in our character, and realize how he prepares us for Christian service. This is understanding the Trinity through practice and not merely focusing on the theory. In so doing, our spirit becomes illuminated and senses through its insight the spiritual reality of God, who transcends the physical world and human reason.

If after reading this book, and finding some of its claims to be logical, you still do not understand the Trinity, don't worry. Simply let yourself be led by God and continue to walk in his path. In the measure that you grow deeper in your relationship with the Father, the Son, and the Holy Spirit, even when you are unable to explain the Trinity completely, you will feel it and understand it in your heart. And what is most important: you will be maintaining a healthy and wonderful life of relationship, service, and fullness with God!

# Appendix
## Toward the Creeds of the Early Church

Theophilus of Antioch was the first person to use the word "trinity" in relation to the Christian faith, around the year AD 180.[1] A short time later the word took the Latin form of *trinitas*. These were the first steps taken to define doctrinally, according to the Injil, the three personal entities (Father, Son, and Holy Spirit) which are seen in the Deity.

Some detractors of the Trinity state that the early Christians did not hold such a doctrine and that no one considered Christ to be God at that time. According to this opinion, the doctrine of the Trinity is the result of the manipulation by the first councils and has nothing to do with biblical teaching.

It is true that the word "trinity" is not found in the biblical texts. This does not mean, however, that the doctrine to which it gives name does not appear clearly in the teaching of the Scriptures. God is "transcendent," "immanent," "omnipresent," etc., even though these truths are not expressed with these same terms in the holy text. But no one denies, as a result, these fundamental attributes of the Divinity. It is simply that these descriptions are the most adequate terms for defining important, revealed truths with very diverse expressions. The same is true for the "Trinity."

In Chapters 4, 5, and 6 of this book, we have verified quite fully that this doctrine does appear and originate in the Bible. And this is the only proof needed to understand that it is a revealed truth. Now is it also true, according to what some people maintain, that the early Christians were unaware of the Trinity? The only way of knowing is to go to the writings of the early thinkers in the church and then see how this doctrine came to be expressed in the creeds, of which the Nicene is the first.

Among the direct disciples of Christ's apostles, some were considered to be pillars of the faith of the early church for their writings in which they reflected the teachings that had become extended and accepted. They are called the apostolic fathers. Some of their names are Clement and Barnabas

---

1 "In like manner also the three days which were before the luminaries, are types of the Trinity, of God, and His Word, and His wisdom." Theophilus of Antioch, *Theophilus to Autolycus*, Book 2, Chapter 15, "Of the Fourth Day." http://www.earlychristianwritings.com/theophilus.html.

(fellow workers of the apostle Paul), and Ignatius and Polycarp (disciples of the apostle John). In their writings we discover above all the following:

- They belong to the interval from AD 90 to 150 after Christ; they contain so many quotes from the New Testament (Injil) that it quite obviously was accepted as sacred text from the very early days.

- Additionally, gathering the New Testament quotes from all Christian literature prior to the Council of Nicaea, we see that they constitute about 95 percent of the Injil. So, even though some maintain that the Injil was intentionally destroyed in Nicaea in AD 325, it would be possible to reconstruct nearly the entire text from these quotations.

- Lastly, at such an early date, the church fathers clearly affirmed that the texts that to our day form the New Testament (Injil) were, according to their criteria, inspired by God.

For example, these words are written by Clement of Rome between AD 95 and 115: "Take up the epistle of the blessed Apostle Paul. What did he write to you at the time when the Gospel first began [to be preached]? Truly, under the inspiration of the Spirit, he wrote to you concerning ..." (The First Epistle of Clement to the Corinthians, 47:1–3).[2]

Another relevant document is the Didache (known as the "Doctrine of the Twelve Apostles"), from a very early date, scarcely forty or fifty years after the death and resurrection of Christ. In addition to containing numerous quotes from the New Testament, we find in it expressions such as these: "as the Lord commanded in his gospel" (8:2) or "as you have it in the gospel of our Lord" (15:4).[3]

In the light of this data, to maintain that the true Injil was done away with by burning it among hundreds of fake copies is simply not common sense for any historian or researcher minimally serious and rigorous. The abundance of documents and references from the first to the third centuries of our era (hundreds of manuscripts and fragments), which include the minutes of the Council of Nicaea, leave no room for doubt. At Nicaea there

---

2   All the quotations of the apostolic fathers are from the online texts available at http://www. earlychristianwritings.com/churchfathers.html and  http://www.preteristarchive.com/Church-History/0070_clement_first.html.

3   http://www.earlychristianwritings.com/text/didache-roberts.html.

was absolutely no attempt to choose one official gospel from among several according to the tastes of the clergy, since the gospel had been spread throughout the empire for a long time. On the contrary, based on the texts that still constitute our gospel today, consensus was given to a formulated definition of the Christian faith—the Nicene Creed.

So then, what did the apostolic fathers think or manifest in their writings about the divinity of Christ and the doctrine of the Trinity?

## The Apostolic Church Fathers and the Trinity

We must remember, first of all, that the purpose of these first writings was not to establish theological definitions. The themes developed in the writings have more to do with how to live the faith and not so much with doctrine. In so doing, however, the apostolic fathers reflected their interpretation of the gospel and, of course, of their understanding of the Divinity. Once again they showed the three persons of the Trinity alongside one another, and unequivocally expressed the divinity of Christ. We don't want to analyze these texts because that would exceed the purpose of this book. Therefore, we have to make do with just quoting the related passages.

### Writings by Clement (AD 95–115)

"Receive our counsel, and you shall be without repentance. For, as God lives, and as the Lord Jesus Christ and the Holy Ghost live,—both the faith and hope of the elect, he who in lowliness of mind, with instant gentleness, and without repentance has observed the ordinances and appointments given by God—the same shall obtain a place and name in the number of those who are being saved through Jesus Christ, through whom is glory to Him for ever and ever. Amen" (Clement to the Corinthians, 50:2).

### Letters by Ignatius of Antioch (AD 105–115)

"There is one Physician who is possessed both of flesh and spirit; both made and not made; God existing in flesh; true life in death; both of Mary and of God; first possible and then impossible, even Jesus Christ our Lord" (Ephesians, 7:2, Roberts-Donaldson English translation).[4]

---

4   http://www.earlychristianwritings.com/text/ignatius-ephesians-roberts.html.

"Being stones of the temple of the Father, prepared for the building of God the Father, and drawn up on high by the instrument of Jesus Christ, which is the cross, making use of the Holy Spirit as a rope" (Ephesians, 9:1).

"Ignorance was removed, and the old kingdom abolished, God Himself being manifested in human form for the renewal of eternal life. And now that took a beginning which had been prepared by God" (Ephesians, 19:3).

"And this will be the case with you if you are not puffed up, and continue in intimate union with Jesus Christ our God" (Trallians, 7:1).

"For our God, Jesus Christ, now that He is with the Father, is all the more revealed [in his glory]. Christianity is not a thing of silence only, but also of [manifest] greatness" (Romans, 3:3).

"For though some would have deceived me according to the flesh, yet the Spirit, as being from God, is not deceived" (Philadelphians, 7:1,2).

"I glorify God, that is Jesus Christ, who has given you such wisdom" (Smyrnaeans, 1:1).

"Being fully persuaded with respect to our Lord, that He was truly of the seed of David according to the flesh, and the Son of God according to the will and power of God; that He was truly born of a virgin" (Smyrnaeans, 1:1,2).

"I pray for your happiness for ever in our God, Jesus Christ, by whom continue ye in the unity and under the protection of God" (Epistle to Polycarp, 8:3).

### Writings by Barnabas (AD 96–98 or 130–140)[5]

"And further, my brethren: if the Lord endured to suffer for our soul, He being Lord of all the world, to whom God said at the foundation of the world, 'Let us make man after our image, and after our likeness,' ...

---

5   Even though in the pseudogospel of Barnabas (an apocryphal work by a Spanish monk who converted to Islam in the fifteenth century) many expressions are put into Jesus' mouth that deny his divinity, in this authentic letter by Barnabas he unquestionably confeses the divinity of Christ.

For if He had not come in the flesh, how could men have been saved by beholding Him?" (Epistle of Barnabas, 5:5,10).[6]

These verses clearly state the following:

1. The Lord that suffered [on the cross, as it is evident in this context] is the Lord of the entire universe!

2. He is the interlocutor with God when God created men saying, "Let Us make man in Our image" (Gen 1:26 MKJ).

3. And it is thanks to the fact that he came in flesh that we may "look" to God's face in order to be saved.

### Epistle to Diognetus (AD 150)
"For, who of men at all understood before His coming what God is?" (Epistle of Mathetes to Diognetus, 8:1).

These are clear and unequivocal declarations with which the apostolic fathers sprinkled their writings. They show us that between the years 90 and 150 of our era—nearly two hundred years prior to the Council of Nicaea—the early Christians understood and believed in the divinity of Christ and the mystery of the Trinity, as is registered in the gospel.

## The Trinity in the Apocryphal Writings
Towards the end of the second century, there were those who started to deny this doctrine, claiming that it was contrary to reason and to the biblical registry. Some accepted only the divinity of the Father. Others, in extreme confusion, presented the three persons almost as three different gods. Others denied the diversity in the Divinity and argued that Father, Son, and Holy Spirit were nothing more than three facets of the same person. But we should understand clearly that, no matter what position is

---

6   The expression "saved by *beholding Him*" is a clear reference to God: "There is no God else beside me; a just God and a Savior; there is none beside me. *Look unto me*, and be ye saved, all the ends of the earth: for I am God, and there is none else" (Isa 45:21,22 KJV, emphasis added). In this quote, Barnabas is showing that Jesus is the same Yahweh as in the verses from the prophet Isaiah, as well as the same God we see in Genesis 1:26.

defended, they all tried to prove their criteria based on the only authoritative source in that regard: the very one and only Injil.[7]

Before the creeds, we can see how this discussion was reflected in some apocryphal texts.[8] Some people, wanting to shed light on the trinitarian discussion, wrote replies to doctrinal deviations; and to give themselves even more authority, they themselves, or other individuals at a later date, attributed their texts to the apostolic fathers. In this way, writings appeared bearing the "signature" of the fathers but that were not penned by them. It can be thought that those who resorted to this tactic were not really seeking to falsify the sources, but rather thought they were reflecting the thoughts or the school of a particular father and therefore attributed to him maybe not the text itself but rather his train of thought. And this is what later gave origin to the false impression that the apostolic fathers had penned these writings.

The most important among these are possibly the apocryphal writings attributed to Ignatius of Antioch, which were used to try and refute the Docetist doctrine. The word "Docetism" comes from the Greek *dokein*, which means "to seem, to appear." According to this heresy—which the Apostle John had already started to confront (see 1 John 4:2,6–8), the body of Christ was not real but rather a type of mirage, an appearance. In addition to this doctrinal deviation, the writing defended the idea that the divine Person who took on human appearance was the Father, or the Son, or the Holy Spirit indistinctly.

The quotes from the Ignatian apocryphal writings transcribed below seek to give answer to these deviations. To do so, they resort to an overly emphatic distinction between Christ—his humanity—and the transcendent and all-powerful God. In these apocrypha, the divinity of Christ is clearly highlighted, but some claims, rather than giving light to the subject, have caused greater confusion. On the one hand they state that

---

7    Some Muslims argue that those who denied the divinity of Christ during the trinitarian discussion age—also categorically denied by Islam—are those who believed and followed the true Gospel. When the trinitarians won, according to them, pertinent changes were made to the text of the true Gospel by the supporters of the Trinity and the original was burned. Those who claim such a thing, however, simply ignore that the trinitarian discussion was never based on different sources, but on different interpretations of the same and only inspired text, accepted by everyone.

8    Apocryphal: a spurious text signed by or attributed to a known author or source in order to give the writing more authority and recognition.

Jesus is "Him that cannot be tempted" (in clear reference to Jas 1:13), that is God himself; but on the other hand they say that the man Jesus, born of Mary, "is not God over all," giving the impression of also denying the divinity of the eternal Son. The purpose is to demonstrate that the body of Christ was not a divine body, nor a mere appearance, but a flesh-and-bone body as human as that of anyone else. An attempt is thus made to avoid the confusion of thinking that Christ's humanity is equal to the nature of the transcendent God. This is why expressions such as these in the Apocrypha cloud the true spiritual identity of Christ, giving the strong impression of contradicting each other.

Some detractors of the Trinity in Turkey use part of these texts to maintain that the fathers rejected that doctrine. This is the reason for including these wide quotes here, although some expressions may cause certain confusion instead of clarifying their views. But after the careful reading of these texts there is not room for doubt insofar as the texts do maintain the divinity of Christ. Being thus, the best is to examine these passages directly.

Transcribed below are all the quotes dealing specifically with the subject of the Divinity in the Ignatian apocrypha, which are the only ones attributed to an apostolic father.[9]

## Ignatian Apocrypha[10]

"There is then one God and Father, and not two or three; One who is; and there is no other besides Him, the only true [God]. For 'the Lord thy God,' saith [the Scripture], 'is one Lord.' And again, 'Hath not one God created us? Have we not all one Father?' And there is also one Son, God the Word. For 'the only-begotten Son,' saith [the Scripture], 'who is in the bosom of the Father.' And again, 'One Lord Jesus Christ.' And in another place, 'What is His name, or what is His Son's name, that we may know?' And there is also one Paraclete. For 'there is also,' saith [the

---

9  We must not confuse the apostolic fathers with the church fathers. The former were direct, first-generation disciples of the apostles and lived in the second half of the first century and the first half of the second. The church fathers, on the other hand, were renowned thinkers, teachers, or theologians during the entire period up to the Eastern and Western Church schism in the eleventh century.

10  The expressions that oppose Docetism and ratify Christ's divinity, his incarnation, or the Trinity, are in bold, and the expressions that appear to be contradictory are in UPPERCASE.

Scripture], 'one Spirit,' since 'we have been called in one hope of our calling.' And again, 'We have drunk of one Spirit,' with what follows. And it is manifest that all these gifts [possessed by believers] 'worketh one and the self-same Spirit.' There are not then either three Fathers, or three Sons, or three Paracletes, but one Father, and one Son, and one Paraclete. Wherefore also the Lord, when He sent forth the apostles to make disciples of all nations, commanded them to 'baptize in the name of the Father, and of the Son, and of the Holy Ghost,' not unto one [person] having three names, nor into three [persons] who became incarnate, but into three possessed of equal honor" (Philippians, 2:1–4).[11]

"For there is but One that became incarnate, and that neither the Father nor the Paraclete, but the Son only, [who became so] not in appearance or imagination, but in reality. For 'the Word became flesh.' For 'wisdom builded for herself a house.' And God the Word was born as man, with a body, of the Virgin, without any intercourse of man. For [it is written], 'A virgin shall conceive in her womb, and bring forth a son.' He was then truly born, truly grew up, truly ate and drank, was truly crucified, and died, and rose again" (Philippians, 3:1,2).

"And how can He be but God, who raises up the dead, sends away the lame sound of limb, cleanses the lepers, restores sight to the blind, and either increases or transmutes existing substances?" (Philippians, 6:1).

"And how, again, does Christ not at all appear to thee to be of the Virgin, but to be God over all, and the Almighty? ... And while you deny that Christ was born, you affirm that the unbegotten[12] was begotten, and that He who had no beginning was nailed to the cross" (Philippians, 7:1,2).

"And thou temptedst the very 'Lord of glory,' ... He who had kept his body from feeling any want for forty days and as many nights, could have also done the same for ever. Why, then, does He suffer hunger? In

---

11   The quotes are from: http://bible.crosswalk.com/History/AD/EarlyChurchFathers/Ante-Nicene/Ignatius/view.cgi?file=anf01-31.htm&size=20. This extensive text is simply seeking to refute the unitarist doctrine that says that God, Jesus, or the Paraclete are the three simultaneously: Father, Son, and Holy Spirit. That is why it insists that each person is untransferable. The last expressions of the paragraph make it clear: "nor into three [persons] who became incarnate, but into three possessed of equal honor"; and in the following paragraph: "And God the Word was born as man."

12   The "unbegotten" is a clear reference to the Father. The Son is the "only begotten." Therefore, what is defended here is not that the Son is not eternal but that it was not the Father who was incarnated.

order to prove that He had assumed a body subject to the same feelings as those of ordinary men. By the first fact He showed that He was God, and by the second that He was also man" (Philippians, 9:3,4).

"If, therefore, thou art trodden down under the feet of the Lord, how dost thou tempt[13] Him that cannot be tempted ... Thou, O Belial, dragon, apostate ... rebel against God, outcast from Christ, alien from the Holy Spirit" (Philippians, 11:1,3).

"I have learned that certain of the ministers of Satan have wished to disturb you, some of them asserting that Jesus was born [only] in appearance, was crucified in appearance, and died in appearance; others that He is not the Son the Creator, and others that HE IS HIMSELF GOD OVER ALL.[14] Others, again, hold that He is a mere man" (Tarsians, 2:1–4).[15]

"Whosoever, therefore, declares that there is but one God, only so as to take away the divinity of Christ, is a devil, and an enemy of all righteousness" (Antiochians, 5:1).[16]

It is therefore clear that the discussion on the divinity of Christ and the unity of the Father, the Son, and the Holy Spirit came about at an early date, in the first generation after the apostles. So the creeds that after years were subsequently formulated are not at all the capricious invention of some religious people but are the unanimous and elaborate response of the church to doctrinal deviations.

The texts quoted in this appendix do not add anything to or take away anything from the truth regarding the Trinity, because this truth is really not based on the declarations of theologians, nor in the subsequent discussion of the church, but in the written revelation of God. The importance of these quotes, however, is that they prove, on the one hand, the commendable efforts to understand, to explore more deeply and to define biblical truth; and on the other hand, they prove the major signifi-

---

13   This is a clear reference to the temptations to which Satan subjected Christ (Matt 4:1–11), and, at the same time, to Christ's divinity, comparing it to James 1:13, "For God cannot be tempted by evil"; stated in this Ignatian Apocrypha with the following expression: "How dost thou tempt Him that cannot be tempted?"

14   By denying that Jesus is God over all, what is actually being denied is not Christ's divinity (as is also understood in the passage), but that his humanity was the very incarnation of the divine substance. According to this, Jesus the man and the transcendent God are not the same thing.

15   http://www.biblestudytools.com/history/early-church-fathers.

16   Ibid.

cance that the doctrine of the Trinity had from the beginning. The creeds are therefore the culmination of all this early work of the church.

We are going to make do with only mentioning the first creeds here, without dealing with the trinitarian discussion of the second and third century or going into the details of this period of doctrinal elaboration, which extended from the apostolic fathers to the first councils. The reason is that these creeds constitute the basis for the statements of faith of all historical churches and for the recognized, standardized, and still valid formulas for the Trinity in our days, and more specifically for those related to the incarnation.

### The Nicene Creed (AD 325)

"We believe in one God, the Father Almighty, Maker of all things visible and invisible. And in one Lord Jesus Christ, the Son of God, begotten of the Father [the only begotten; that is, of the essence of the Father, God of God], Light of Light, very God of very God, begotten, not made, being of one substance with the Father; by whom all things were made [both in heaven and on earth]; who for us men, and for our salvation, came down and was incarnate and was made man; he suffered, and the third day he rose again, ascended into heaven; from thence he shall come to judge the quick and the dead. And in the Holy Ghost."[17]

### The Apostles' Creed (AD 340)

"I believe in God, the Father Almighty, Maker of heaven and earth: And in Jesus Christ, his only Son our Lord: Who was conceived by the Holy Ghost, Born of the Virgin Mary: Suffered under Pontius Pilate, Was crucified, dead, and buried: He descended into hell; The third day he rose again from the dead: He ascended into heaven, And sitteth on the right hand of God the Father Almighty: From thence he shall come to judge the quick and the dead. I believe in the Holy Ghost: The holy Catholic Church: The Communion of Saints: The Forgiveness of sins; The Resurrection of the body, And the Life everlasting. Amen."[18]

---

17   http://en.wikipedia.org/wiki/Nicene_Creed.
18   http://www.creeds.net/ancient/apostles.htm.

## The Chalcedonian Creed (AD 451)

"Therefore, following the holy fathers, we all with one accord teach men to acknowledge one and the same Son, our Lord Jesus Christ, at once complete in Godhead and complete in manhood, truly God and truly man, consisting also of a reasonable soul and body; of one substance with the Father as regards his Godhead, and at the same time of one substance with us as regards his manhood; like us in all respects, apart from sin; as regards his Godhead, begotten of the Father before the ages, but yet as regards his manhood begotten, for us men and for our salvation, of Mary the Virgin, the God-bearer; one and the same Christ, Son, Lord, Only-begotten, recognized in two natures, without confusion, without change, without division, without separation; the distinction of natures being in no way annulled by the union, but rather the characteristics of each nature being preserved and coming together to form one person and subsistence, not as parted or separated into two persons, but one and the same Son and Only-begotten God the Word, Lord Jesus Christ; even as the prophets from earliest times spoke of him, and our Lord Jesus Christ himself taught us, and the creed of the fathers has handed down to us."[19]

# Conclusion

The true importance of such a lengthy dissertation is to be able to establish an authentic, deep, and practical relationship with God as Father, Son, and Holy Spirit. The good news of the Injil is that:

*"God was in Christ reconciling the world to Himself... As God said, 'I will dwell in them and walk among them'" (2 Cor 5:19; 6:16 NASB).*

Even though we may not understand how electricity works, we see that—thanks to its power, light, and heat—it can make our lives so much easier. In the case of the Trinity, the goal is to deepen our relationship with God.

In the same way that we cannot see the power of electricity itself with our natural eyes, nor touch it with our bare hands:

- As creatures secluded within the confines of space and time, we are incapable of understanding or reaching the Divinity.

---

19 http://www.reformed.org/documents/chalcedon.html.

- As the imperfect beings and sinners that we are, we cannot approach the perfect God without being consumed by his holiness.

What happens on falling into a fire? We are blinded by that light that in its purest power annuls any residue of shadow. Such is the transcendence and holiness of God the Father:

> *"He who is the blessed and only Sovereign, the King of kings and Lord of lords, who alone has immortality, who dwells in unapproachable light, whom no one has ever seen or can see. To him be honor and eternal dominion. Amen" (2 Tim 6:15,16 ESV).*

> *"Every good thing given and every perfect gift is from above, coming down from the Father of lights, with whom there is no variation or shifting shadow" (Jas 1:17 NASB).*

But God wanted to light the path that best leads to him. He has revealed himself to humankind in the most perfect fashion: he prepared a message on the level of our understanding, a way that we could approach him without being consumed. The visible form of the energy is light.

> *"The Son is the radiance of God's glory and the exact representation of his being, sustaining all things by his powerful word" (Heb 1:3).*

> *"Christ, who is the image of God" (2 Cor 4:4).*

> *"He is the image of the invisible God" (Col 1:15).*

Jesus said to them: "I am the light of the world" (John 8:12; 1:4,9; 3:19; 9:5; 12:46; etc.).

The God who is "light" (1 John 1:5) created a "covering" for himself to enter this world; he became incarnated. The humanity of Christ is not divine, but the Spirit and the Word that live in him and constitute his personality are indeed God, the Son of God. This is how we are able to "see" the invisible God.

> *"No one has seen God at any time; the only begotten God who is in the bosom of the Father, He has explained Him" (John 1:18 NASB).*

> *"The mystery of godliness is great: God appeared in a body" (1 Tim 3:16).*

> *"For in Christ all the fullness of the Deity lives in bodily form" (Col 2:9).*

Jesus not only illuminates the way to God but has also settled the debt of our sins that separated us from the holy God. He has dispelled the darkness! Finally, the way to God is definitely open!

> *"God was in Christ reconciling the world to Himself ... He made Him who knew no sin to be sin on our behalf, so that we might become the righteousness of God in Him" (1 Cor 5:19, 21).*

On the cross, God "condemned sin in the flesh" (Rom 8:3).

> *"For God so loved the world, that He gave His only begotten Son, that whoever believes in Him shall not perish, but have eternal life" (John 3:16 NASB).*

Here we have the gospel, the good news. God is love. He was love in eternity; he created the world out of love; and even though we rebel against him, he continues to love us. About two thousand years ago he entered our world by becoming a man. Sin, the cause of eternal separation between God and man, is something so offensive and loathsome to his eyes that the only way we could be freed from its power and consequences and be received into his love was through the death of an innocent victim. And he sacrificed that which was most valuable: the infinite life of the incarnate Word! Now he invites us to freely accept the gift of forgiveness and of love. Not in exchange for a series of good religious works—as if we could bribe him—but by choosing to follow him in response to a definite surrender of our former, self-seeking way of living. Because he is the first one who relinquished his position in favor of you and me!

We do not dare touch a high-voltage electrical cable with our bare hands. In the same way the light that electricity produces helps us to see and we are warmed by its heat, so the warmth of the Spirit can melt the coldest of lives without God.

When you give your life to Jesus Christ, you receive the Holy Spirit in your heart. However, a person's heart must first be purified from the aftereffects of sin. As long as the heart is not sanctified or made holy—not by one's own efforts but by the blood of Christ, the one who is Holy cannot come to live in it. That is why we must repent, make an about face with regards to how we have been living, believing in, and committing ourselves to Christ.

Once the matter of sin and its eternal punishment has been resolved, God has also provided us with the strength necessary to live a life that truly pleases him. Once again, it is the Holy Spirit who prompts us, as believers, from inside of us, to live clean, God-honoring, and worthwhile lives.

The Holy Spirit is who facilitates contact and fellowship between the divine and human dimensions! Once this contact occurs, he reproduces the image of Christ in the believer who obeys and serves him. And this, not from personal merit but as grace given to the person who accepts it with humility.

> *"But he who unites himself with the Lord is one with him in spirit"*
> *(1 Cor 6:17).*

> *"Don't you know that you yourselves are God's temple and that God's Spirit lives in you?" (1 Cor 3:16).*

> *"Now the Lord is the Spirit, and where the Spirit of the Lord is, there is freedom. And we, who with unveiled faces all reflect the Lord's glory, are being transformed into his likeness with ever-increasing glory, which comes from the Lord, who is the Spirit"*
> *(2 Cor 3:17,18).*

In this way, the Holy Spirit creates a closeness and maximum intimacy between the believer and God. So if we do not know God as the triune God, it is impossible to know his love in the Father, his grace and forgiveness in the Son, and his fellowship in the Holy Spirit.

> *"May the grace of the Lord Jesus Christ, and the love of God, and the fellowship of the Holy Spirit be with you all" (2 Cor 13:14).*

The very moment we repent—turn away from ourselves and turn to God, giving our lives over to him—and believe in the sufficiency of the atoning death of Christ for our salvation, "how much more will your Father in heaven give the Holy Spirit to those who ask him!" (Luke 11:13).

In summary, until *'Issa al-Masih* [20] returns to earth, our reason for living is to worship and pray to God as Father, to give ourselves to Christ as Lord, and to receive strength to walk in his path by being joined to the Holy

---

20  *'Issa al-Masih,* Jesus the Messiah. The return of Jesus Christ to earth before the Day of Judgment is also a belief well extended among the Muslims.

Spirit. It is the Holy Spirit who applies the value of the atoning death of Christ and his righteousness to our own lives, so that we might follow in his footsteps and be transformed into his likeness. For a committed believer, the only reason to live is to please the Father, follow the Son, and live in the power of the Holy Spirit.

No one has ever seen God nor can see him in his pure state, in his essence. But thanks to the living Word—the *Kalamu'llah*—we can not only hear him but also see him "live." And thanks to the action of the Holy Spirit in our lives, who etches his eternal life and his will onto the believer's heart, we can also "feel him."

This is the Trinity: Being, Word, and Spirit. The Creator, Savior, and Sanctifier of every person and who has been revealed as Father, Son, and Holy Spirit.

Such a relationship with God is not achieved by changing one's religion. Jesus Christ did not call people to become "Christians." It is not a matter of belonging to one religion or another but of establishing a living and personal relationship with God, through his Word and through his Spirit. It is about giving oneself to God in true submission (Islam) and in conscious faith.

Because Jesus is the one who said: "I am the way and the truth and the life. No one comes to the Father except through me" (John 14:6).

## Romanization according to ALA-LC* (1997)
**American Library Association–Library of Congress**

| Arabic | Rom. | Arabic | Rom. |
|---|---|---|---|
| ء - hamza | -, ʼ | ع- ayn | ʻ |
| ا - alif | a | غ - ghayn | gh |
| ب - ba | b | ف - fa | f |
| ت - ta | t | ق - qaf | q |
| ث - tha | th | ك - kaf | k |
| ج - jim | j | ل - lam | l |
| ح - ha | ḥ | م - mim | m |
| خ - kha | kh | ن - nun | n |
| د - dal | d | ه - ha | h |
| ذ - dhal | dh | و - waw | u, w* |
| ر - ra | r | ي - ya | i, y* |
| ز - zay | z | آ - ʼalif | āʻ, ā |
| س - sin | s | ة - ta | h, t |
| ش - shin | sh | ى - alif maqshura | y, - |
| ص - sad | ṣ | ﻻ - lam alif | lā |
| ض - dad | ḍ | ﻻ - alif lam | al-, a#- |
| ط - tah | ṭ | * when are used as a consonant | |
| ظ - zah | ẓ | # instead of "l," pronounce the next consonant | |

***abad,*** أبد, **or** ***abadi,*** أبدي: Eternal, sempiternal, without end; as distinguished from *ʼazal* (أزل), "without beginning" (Hughes, *Dictionary of Islam*).

**Abu Bakr,** أبو بكر: Muhammad's father-in-law and one of his closest companions (*sahaba:* صحابة) and advisers. He succeeded the Prophet's political and administrative functions, thereby initiating the office of the caliphate.

***ahlu'l-Kitab,*** أهل الكتاب: The "people of the Book," or those in possession of the inspired Word of God, as Jews or Christians.

***ahlu'l-sunnah,*** أهل السُّنَّة: Qualified lawyers (i.e., preservers of the *Sunnah*); "the people of the Path." *Sunnah* (سنة): lit., "path, way, manner of life." A term used in the religion of the Muslim to express the custom or manner of life—the tradition which records either the sayings or doings of Muhammad. Consequently, all traditional law is divided into: 1) *Sunnatu'l-Fi'l*, what Muhammad did; 2) *Sunnatu'l-Qaul*, what Muhammad enjoined; and 3) *Sunnatu'l-Taqrir*, that which was done or said in the presence of Muhammad, and which was not forbidden by him (Hughes, *Dictionary of Islam*).

**Ahmadiyya:** A religious movement founded towards the end of the nineteenth century and originating with the life and teachings of Mirza Ghulam Ahmad (1835–1908). He claimed that he was the Mujaddid (divine reformer) of the fourteenth Islamic century, the promised Messiah and Mahdi awaited by Muslims.

*al-Asma-Allah-ul-Husna,* الأسماء الله الحسنى: Allah's most beautiful names.

*al-Asma-ul-Husna,* الأسماء الحسنى: The most beautiful names.

*'alim,* عَالِم: Wise, wiseman. Term used to designate the scholars in Islamic religion, philosophy, or legal issues.

**Apocrypha:** Hidden, esoteric, spurious, of questionable authenticity; Christian texts that are not canonical. The general term is usually applied to the books that the Christian church considered useful but not divinely inspired. From the Greek (ἀπόκρυφα: those having been hidden away).

*'aqnum,* الاقنوم, **pl.** *aqanim,* اقانيم: Hypostasis. According to Muslim lexicographers, it is a word which means the root or principle of a thing and, according to the *Naṣārā* (Nazarenes), there are three *aqanim*; namely, *wujud* (entity or substance), *hayath* (life), and *'ilm* (knowledge); and also, *Ab* (Father), *Ibn* (Son), and *Ruhu'l-Qudus* (Holy Spirit). It is also the name of a book amongst the Nazarenes which addresses these three (Hughes, *Dictionary of Islam*).

**Ash'arites,** *al-ash'airah,* الأشاعرة: A school of early Muslim speculative theology founded by the theologian Abu al-Hasan al-Ash'ari (d. AH 324/AD 936). In contrast to the Mu'tazilite school of Islamic theology, the Ash'arite view was that comprehension of the unique nature and characteristics of God was beyond human capability.

**Athari:** A school that derives its name from the Arabic word *athar,* meaning "narrations." The Athari methodology is to avoid delving into extensive theological speculation. They use the Qur'an, the Sunnah, and sayings of the Sahaba (Companions of the Prophet).

**attribute:** Abstraction of a characteristic of an entity or substance. Aspect of God's character, description of what God is, quality inherent to the divine substance or essence. In respect to the divine attributes, Ash'arites believe that God acts—i.e., is powerful—through his attributes (*Allah qadir bi-qudratih*).

*aya,* آية; **pl.** *ayat,* آيات: Verse, of the Qur'an.

*'azal,* أزل: Eternity with respect to the past; as distinguished from *abad* (أبد), "eternity without end" (Hughes, *Dictionary of Islam*).

*'azali,* أزلي: Preeternal, outdating time.

**begotten, only:** The "only begotten" is the Son, as he emanates from the bosom of the Father. This "birth" is spiritual and timeless, therefore has nothing to do with a "creation" or with "procreation."

**conscience:** This term is used related to the persons of the Trinity in the sense of the consciousness or awareness of oneself, as opposed to the others; the awareness that each one of the divine Persons coexist with the others as differentiated beings.

*dhat,* ذات: Essence, self. *Adh-dhat*: the essence in the absolute meaning of the word, the ultimate reality to which all qualities relate (Hughes, *Dictionary of Islam*). Even though one of the meanings of *dhat* is the English "self" and *bi-dhat* (بذات) means "in self," in Arabic the equivalence between "*dhat*" and the English meaning of "person" is not so strong. On the other hand the Arabic word for "person" is *shakhs* (شخص). But this could be understood as the physical entity of the person, not only as the physical one, and this may create a great confusion if it is used for defining the Trinity.

However, in Islamic theology the names by which Allah is known can be divided in two main categories: 1) the names of the qualities (*al-asm-adh-dhat*), such as Allah and ar-Rahman, and 2) the names of the qualities (*al-asma-as-sifat*) such as ar-Rahim and al-Bari. Building a bridge between these concepts, we may say that *dhat*, understood as "self-identity," is useful as the term that includes the "personal" aspects of the divine Being and *wujud* as the one which emphasizes the "substantial" aspects.

**Docetism:** From the Greek *dokeo* (δοκέω, to seem). The belief that Jesus' physical body was an illusion, as was his crucifixion; that is, Jesus only *seemed* to have a physical body and to physically die, but in reality he was incorporeal, a pure spirit, and hence could not physically die.

**entropy:** The name given to the second law of thermodynamics, which states that everything in the universe has a tendency to move towards disorder.

**epistemology:** From the Greek *episteme* (ἐπιστήμη, knowledge, science) + *logos* (λόγος, science, study, theory). The branch of philosophy concerned with the nature and scope (limitations) of knowledge. Among others it addresses the question: "How do we know what we know?"

**ferd, فرد:** Individual.

**generation:** The "generation" of the divine Word is not a physical birth. The divine Word (the Son) is being "begotten" in the essence of God from eternity. That is, he "emanates" from God, but this generating act is not in the physical sense. Without a doubt, God does not procreate nor is he procreated. This generation is not an act of creation either, because it occurs in eternity and in the bosom of the Divinity, not outside of it.

**ghayr, غير:** Other, distinct.

**ghayr mtsaw, غير متساو:** Unequal, unlike.

**hadith, حديث:** Statement or action attributed to the Prophet.

**Hadith Qudsi, أحاديث قدسية:** Holy sayings (of the Prophet but not part of the Qur'an).

**hamd, حمد:** Praised.

**Hanbalites, al-hanbaliyya, الحَنْبَلِي:** Scholars who study the connection between the Qur'an and the *Sunnah* (in the hadiths). Hanbalites are adherents to the theology of Ahmad ibn Hanbal (AH 164–241/AD 780–855). One of the four Islamic law schools, which fought against the rationalist Mu'tazilah school. Hanbalites believe that God is eternal with his power and light and that he speaks, knows, and creates eternally.

**haqiqah, حقيقة:** Truth, reality, essence, sincerity.

**Haqq, حقّ:** True, truth, justice, right. By the Sufi mystics it is used for the divine essence. *Al-Haqq* is one of the ninety-nine attributes of Allah (Hughes, *Dictionary of Islam*).

**hayy wahiy, حي وحي:** Living revelation. Used in this book in reference to the *kalam nafsi*, i.e., the breath of the Word, synonymous with the Logos.

**hikmat, حِكْمَة:** Wisdom.

*ḥikmatu'llahi,* حكمة الله: Wisdom of God.

**hypostasis:** From the Greek *hypostasis* (ὑπόστασις, that which stands beneath). In early Christian writings it is used to denote "being" or "substantive reality" and is not always distinguished in meaning from *ousia* (οὐσία, essence); it was used in this way by Tatian and Origen, and also in the Nicene Creed of 325. As "hypostatic union," the term is used to describe the union of Christ's humanity and divinity.

*ibadah,* عِبَادَةٌ, pl. *ibadat* عِبَادَات: Worship, fellowship, devotion. According to Muslim doctors, *ash-Shari'iah* (the Law) may be divided into five sections: *I'tiqādāt* (belief); *Ādāb* (moralities); *'Ibādāt* (devotions); *Mu'āmalāt* (transactions); and *'Uqūbāt* (punishments) (Hughes, *Dictionary of Islam*).

*Ibnu'llah,* أبن الله, or *Ibn Allah*: Son of God. The Bible refers to *Ibnu'llah* in a spiritual sense, and it does not mean *waladu'llah* (وَلَدُ الله, blood son of Allah), which would have a physical or biological sense.

*'ilm,* عِلْم: Knowledge, science.

**immanence:** Philosophical and metaphysical theories of divine presence which hold that some divine being or essence manifests in and through all aspects of the material world. From the Latin *in manere* (to remain within). In contrast with transcendence.

**imminence:** The quality of being imminent, i.e., about to occur. In this work the concept is used to refer to the Second Person of the Trinity, in contrast with the transcendence of God the Father and the immanence of the Holy Spirit, focusing on the entries of the Son into the world.

**immutability:** In theology, the idea of God's immutability is essentially tied to God's eternality. God, being outside of time (transtemporal), cannot change because he is not affected by time, which is the agent of change in a temporal universe.

**Injil,** إنجيل: Gospel or New Testament (sometimes the whole Bible). Greek *evangelion* (εὐαγγέλιον). Injil is used in the Qur'an, in the popular narrative (*riwayah:* رِوَايَة), and in all Muhammadan theological works of an early date, for the revelations made by God to Jesus. But in recent works it is applied by Muhammadans to the New Testament (Hughes, *Dictionary of Islam*).

*'Issa al-Masih,* عيسى المسيح, or *Yasua'al-Masih,* يسُوعَ المسيح: 'Issa the Messiah or Jesus the Christ.

*jawhar,* جوهر: Essence.

*kalam lafzi,* كلام لَفْظِي: Pronounced word.

*kalam nafsi,* كلام نفسي: Essence of the word (of God).

*Kalamu'llah,* كَلامُ الله, or *Kalimat'ullahi,* كَلِمَةُ الله: Word of God or divine Word. Additionally: *kalimatuhu minhu,* كَلِمَة مِنْهُ, "a word from Him" (Al 'Imran 3:39); *kalimatuhu minhu'llahi,* كَلِمَة مِنَ اللّٰه, "a word from God" (Al 'Imran 3:45); *Allahi wakalimatuhu,* الله وَكَلِمَتُهُ, "God and His word" (An-Nisa 4:171); All of these terms refer to Jesus Christ and his birth.

*Kitabu'l-mukaddes,* كِتَابُ ٱلْمُقَدَّسْ: Holy Book (i.e., the Bible).

*kun fayakunu,* كُنْ فَيَكُونُ: [Allah says,] "'Be,' and it is" (Al 'Imran 3:47).

*lawhin mahfuzin,* لَوْحٍ مَحْفُوظٍ: Preserved tablet (Al-Buruj 85:22).

**Logos:** Greek term translated as "Word" in John 1:1. It refers to the thought and Word of God—sometimes identified with his wisdom (cf. Proverbs 8) which he possessed from eternity, through whom he created all things and spoke to the prophets, and who manifested himself in the incarnation of the Son as Jesus (cf. John 1:1–3,14; Hebrews 1:1; 1 Peter 1:10,11).

*Mahdi,* مهدي: The Guide; a figure who Muslims believe will appear with Jesus before the end of time.

*makhluq,* مخلوق: Creature (i.e., created).

*Masih,* مسيح: The (biblical) Messiah, Jesus Christ.

**Maturidites,** *al-maturidiyyah,* الماتريدي: Followers of al-Maturidi, Abu Mansur Muhammad (AH 333/AD 944), founder of an important school of orthodox, conservative theology which admitted a place for human reason but not a paramount one. The most substantial difference between Ash'arites and Maturidites was the former's emphasis on the absolute power of the will of Allah, and the latter's emphasis that humans have freedom and responsibility.

**Mujassimah,** مجسمة or **Mushabbiha,** مشبهة: Said that Allah has a sort of material existence. Some allege that Allah has body, literally possesses hands, hearing, and sight according to the verses in the Qur'an that use those 'corporal' expressions referring to Allah (Cf. Hud 11:37; Al-Qasas 28:88; Az-Zumar 39:67; Al-Fath 48:10; Ar-Rahman 55:26,27).

*mumin,* مؤمن: Believer.

*mumkin al-wujud bi'l-dhatihi,* ممكن الوجود بالذاته: Existent in itself, one who has existence in himself. Here we see two relevant aspects that are present in Jehovah's name as well: the "I" and the "am" (i.e., identity and existence, in the biblical definition), "existence" and "selfness" (in the Islamic definition); pointing out the two basic aspects that allow us to understand the diversity in the divine unity—a diversity of "selves" (three identities) sharing a unity of existence (one unique being).

*mundemij,* مندمج: Immanent, merged.

*murid,* مُرِيد: One who wills (i.e., sovereign).

**Murji'ah:** Followers are called Murjites or Murji'ites. Emerged as a theological school opposed to the Kharijites (those who went out, i.e., dissidents). They advocated that only God can judge who is a true Muslim and who is not, and no one else can judge another as an infidel (*kafir*). This theology promoted tolerance of the Umayyad dynasty and converts to Islam who appeared halfhearted in their obedience.

*mutakallim,* مُتَكَلِّم: One who speaks.

**Mu'tazilis, *al-mu'tazilah,*** المعتزلة: A distinct Islamic school of speculative theology that flourished in the cities of Basra and Baghdad during the eighth to tenth centuries. It is still adopted by a small, dispersed minority of Muslim intellectuals. Adherents are usually not accepted by Sunni scholars due to the Mu'tazili belief that human reason is more reliable than tradition. Because of this belief, Mu'tazilis tend to interpret passages of the Qur'an farther from their literal meanings than other Muslims, a practice frowned upon by many Sunni scholars. The theology of the Mu'tazilis concerning the nature of God has influenced Shi'a Islam and has been partly integrated into the theology of the Imami Shiism. In respect to the divine attributes, Mu'tazilis believe that God acts—i.e., knows—by his essence (*Allah 'alim bi-dhatih*).

*mute'aal,* متعال: Transcendent.

*nafs,* نفس: Breath, soul.

**New Testament:** The name given to the second major division of the Christian Bible, the first such division being the much longer Old Testament. Greek: *Kainē Diathēkē* (Καινη Διαθήκη, New Testament); Arabic: *Ahdi Jadid* (عهد جديد, New Covenant).

***Nuru'llahi,*** نُورُ اللّٰه: Light of God.

**Old Testament:** The collection of books that forms the first of the two-part Christian biblical canon. Judaism uses the term *Tanakh* to refer to its canon of the Masoretic Text. Arabic: *Ahdi Atiq* (عهد عتيق, Old Covenant).

**ontology:** From the Greek *ontos* (ὄντος, being) + *logia* (λογία, science, study, theory). The philosophical study of the nature of being, existence, or reality in general, as well as the basic categories of being and their relations. Traditionally listed as a part of the major branch of philosophy known as metaphysics, ontology deals with questions concerning what entities exist or can be said to exist, and how such entities can be grouped.

**person:** When referring to God in Western theology, "person" points out the three diverse identities revealed within the Divinity. In the early church times Christians searched for appropriate language prior to the formation of the creeds. In the Greek culture speaking about "persona" meant at that time what "character" means in theater today, thus an "individual." Therefore, Greeks preferred to use "hypostasis," i.e., "other level of existence," to refer to the Father, to the Son, and to the Holy Spirit. On the other hand, when it came into usage in the West through the Latin-speaking theologians, "person" became the word for distinguishing different "identities" within the Divinity without being confused with different "individuals," thereby not allowing a tritheistic comprehension when the term is used related to the Trinity. The normal Arabic word for "person" is *shakhs* and does not correspond with the theological meaning of its English translation. Whereas in English among several meanings we find the "identity" of a being, in Arabic it is understood specifically as a "human being." The Arab Christian theologians largely used *'aqnum*, pl. *aqanim*, as the equivalent for the Greek *hypostasis* which the Greeks in their wisdom determined was the best term for Father, Son, and Holy Spirit. The medieval Muslim theologians were well aware of this usage.

**procreate:** Expresses biological reproduction, as opposed to "generate" in theology, and in contrast with the spiritual conception of the Son—the

Word—in the God's bosom.

*qadim,* قديم: Ancient, without beginning, eternal.

*qadir,* قَدِير: Powerful, able.

*Al-Qur'an Al-kerim,* القرآن الكريم: Holy Qur'an.

*Rabb,* رب: Lord.

*rahim,* رحيم: Merciful.

*rasul,* رسول: Messenger, prophet.

**revelation:** In theology, the disclosing or making something obvious through active or passive divine communication. While in Christian faith revelation may come as an inspiration to the heart of the prophets, the Islamic view is that Allah dictated literally his words to Muhammad.

*riwayah,* رواية: Transmission, narrative, account.

*ruh,* روح: Spirit.

*Ruhu'llah,* روح الله: Spirit of God.

*Ruhu'l-Qudus,* رُوحُ القُدُس: Holy Spirit.

**The Seven Essential Attributes:** *Hayy,* حي, Living One; *'Alim,* عليم, Knower; *Sami',* سميع, Hearer; *Basir,* بَصير, Observer; *Qadir,* قَدِير, Powerful; *Murid,* مورِيد, Willer; *Mutakallim,* متكلم, Speaker.

*shakhs,* شخص: Person, human being.

**Shi'a:** They believe in the political and religious leadership of imams from the progeny of Ali ibn Abi Talib, who according to most Shi'a are in a state of *ismah,* meaning "infallibility." Shi'a Islam has several branches, the largest of which is the Twelvers. Other smaller groups include the Ismaili and Zaidi.

*shirk,* شرك: Sin of association, to make any creature equal to Allah. Idolatry, paganism, polytheism, ascribing plurality to the Deity. Associating anything with God (Hughes, *Dictionary of Islam*).

*sifat adh-dhatiyya,* صفات الذاتية: Intrinsic attributes.

*sifat an-nafsiyyah,* صفات النفسية: Essential attributes.

*sifat-e-thubutiyyah,* صفات ثبوتية: Positive attributes.

**The Six Intrinsic Attributes of the Divinity (*As-Sifat adh-Dhatiyya*):** *al-Wujud*, existence; *al-Qidam*, being without beginning, and eternal in the past; *al-Baqa'*, being without end, and eternal in the future; al-Wahdaniyya, having no partner or match; *al-Mukhalafatu li'l-hawadith*, being dissimilar to every creature in every respect; *al-Qiyamu bi nafsihi*, self-existence or not needing anything for his existence. No creature has any of these six attributes, nor any relation with them. They belong to Allah exclusively. Some Muslim scholars say that *al-Mukhalafatu li'l-hawadith* and *al-Wahdaniyya* are the same, and that *as-Sifat adh-Dhatiyya* are five.

**Sufism:** Not strictly a denomination, Sufism is a mystical-ascetic form of Islam. Sufis strive to obtain direct experience of God by making use of "intuitive and emotional faculties" that one must be trained to use. Most Sufi orders, or *tariqas*, can be classified as either Sunni or Shi'a.

**Sunni:** Sunni Islam is the largest branch of Islam, comprising at least 85 percent of the world's 1.5 billion Muslims. The word "Sunni" comes from the word "Sunnah," which means the words and actions or example of Muhammad (see *ahlu'l-sunnah*). Sunni are distinguished from other Muslims by their dependency on the hadiths (i.e., the sayings of the prophet), especially those compiled by Sahih al-Bukhari and Sahih Muslim. There are four Sunni schools of law (*madh'hab*): Hanafi, Maliki, Shafi'i, and Hanbali, which reflect different opinions on some laws and obligations.

***surah***, سورة: Chapter of the Qur'an.

***tafsir***, تفسير: Exegesis, interpretation, explanation.

***tanzil***, تَنْزِل: To send down, to descend. According to Islamic theology it refers to the revealed, divine text that descended from heaven to Muhammad. Rarely has it been suggested by Islamic scholars that the *tanzil* of Christianity is in the person of Jesus himself as the Messenger of God and his Word (*Kelimatuh*; An-Nisa 4:171) (Glassé, *New Encyclopedia of Islam* [Revelation]).

***tathlith***, تَثْلِيث: Triad or trinity. The Trinity is erroneously designated using the term *tathlith*, that is, "triad," by Islamic theological circles. Therefore the correct equivalent of its definition would be: *tathlith fi'l-tauhid*, تثليث في التوحيد, triad in the unity (i.e., three in one).

*tauhid,* توحيد: A term used to express the unity of the Godhead, which is the great fundamental basis of the religion of Muhammad (Hughes, *Dictionary of Islam* [God]). It comes from a similar root as "one" (*echâd,* אחד) in Deuteronomy 6:4—"Hear, O Israel: The LORD our God, the LORD is one."

**Taurat,** توراة: The title given in the Qur'an (Al-Imran 3:2), and in all Muhammadan works, for the books of Moses. It is the Hebrew Torah (תּוֹרָה), "the Law" (Hughes, *Dictionary of Islam*).

transcendent: Its first meaning, as part of the concept pair transcendence-immanence, is used primarily with reference to God's relation to the world. Here "transcendent" means that God is completely outside of and beyond the world, as contrasted with the notion that God is manifested in the world.

**Trinity:** From the Latin *"trinitas,"* meaning "the number three, a triad"; later was developed as a combination of "tres in uno," i.e., "three in unity." Thus, the concept of one God revealed in three persons: Father, Son, and Holy Spirit.

*'ulama,* عُلَمَا ء: Islamic scholars.

*wahdat,* وحدة: One, unit; that is, an indivisible and homogeneous unit.

*wahiy,* وحي: Revelation, inspiration, oracle. The concept of the inspiration of the Qur'an, in contrast with the biblical understanding; doesn't include any implication of the prophets, who are merely mechanical receivers of God's revelation. It is closer to the concept of an oracle; a divine utterance delivered to man.

*wasf,* وَصْف: Quality, characteristic, description.

*wujud,* وُجُود: Existence, presence, being.

**Zabur,** زبور: Psalms. From the Hebrew *zimrāh* (זמרה, psalm, chant) (Ps 81:2; 98:5). The title given to the Psalms of David—in the Qur'an—where it occurs only three times (An-Nisa' 4:161; Bani Isra'il 17:57; Ta Ha 21:105) (Hughes, *Dictionary of Islam*).

**Zahiri:** A school of thought which literally translates as "literalist," regarded as heterodox among many Muslims for rejecting *qiyas* (analogical reasoning) and arguing that Allah's anthropomorphic attributes were to be regarded as literal (i.e., that Allah actually has hands in Al-Ma'idah 5:64).

*zuhur,* ظهور: Appearance.

# BIBLIOGRAPHY

Abdulahad, Dâvud. *Tevrat ve İncil'e göre Hz. Muhammed (A. S.)* [Muhammad according to the Old and New Testament]. Istanbul: Nil Yayınları, 1992.

Ataurrahim, Muhammed. *Bir İslâm Peygamberi: Hz. İsa* [Jesus: An Islamic prophet]. Istanbul: Baskı, İnsan Yayınları, 1983.

Aydin, Mahmut. *İsâ: Tanrı mı, İnsan mı?* [Is Jesus God or man?]. Istanbul: İZ Yayıncılık, 2002.

Bromiley, Geoffrey W. *International Standard Bible Encyclopedia.* Grand Rapids, MI: Eerdmans, 1986.

Brother Mark. *A "Perfect" Qur'an, or "So It Was Made to Appear to Them"? A Response to Islamic Allegations concerning the Gospel, the Qur'an and the Islam.* n.p.: Brother Mark, 2000.

Davud, Abdulahad. "Mahoma: Según el Antiguo y Nuevo Testamento." In *Muhammad in the Bible.* Al-Kitab Publications, 1991.

Douglas, J. D. *Nuevo Diccionario Biblico Certeza* [New Certeza biblical dictionary]. Barcelona: Certeza 2000.

Dursun, Turan. *Allah.* İstanbul: Kaynak Yayınları, 1993.

Ekinci, Lütfi. *Kitab-ı Mukaddes Allah'ın Sözü müdür?* [Is the Bible the Word of God?]. Istanbul: Müjde Yayıncılık, 1993.

Glassé, Cyril. *The New Encyclopedia of Islam: A Revised Edition of the Concise Encyclopedia of Islam*, Lanham, MD: AltaMira Press, 2002.

Haley, John W., and Santiago Escuain. *Diccionario de Dificultades y Aparentes Contradicciones Bíblicas* [Dictionary of difficulties and apparent contradictions in the Bible]. Barcelona: Clie, 1998.

Hughes, Thomas Patrick. *A Dictionary of Islam.* London: W. H. Allen, 1895.

Johnson, Steve A. "Ibn Sina's Fourth Ontological Argument for God's Existence." *The Muslim World* 74 (1984): iii–iv, 161–71.

*Kutsal Kitap* [The Holy Bible]. Istanbul: Yeni Yaşam Yayınları, 2000.

Lacueva, Francisco. *Curso de Formación Teológica Evangélica.* Vol. 2, *Un Dios en Tres Personas.* Barcelona: Clie, 1982.

———. *Curso de Formación Teológica Evangélica.* Vol. 4, *La Persona y la Obra de Jesucristo.* Barcelona: Clie, 1984.

———. *Nuevo Testamento Interlineal Griego-Español.* Barcelona: Clie, 1982.

Mir, Jose. *Tanrı'nın Telefon Numarası: Gelişen Vahiy Yolları Üzerine Bir Çalışma* [God's phone number: Essay on the growing ways of revelation]. Istanbul: Lütuf Yayıncılık, 1993.

Mısri Divanı, Niyazi ve Şerhi. *Sohbet ile Şerheden Pir Seyyid Muhammed Nur.* Istanbul: Hakikat Bilgisi, 2003.

*The Qur'an.* Turkish translation by Meâl. Ankara: Ministry of Religious Affairs, 1985.

Ruiz Bueno, Daniel. *Padres Apostólicos* [Apostolic fathers]. Catholic edition. Madrid: Bilingüe Completa, 1950.

Shirazi, Hassan, الأحاديث القدسية, *Al-Hadith Al-Qudsi, A Word Of Allah,* Translated by S. M. Zaki Baqri. Qum: Ansariyan, 2003.

Strong, James. *Strong's Greek Dictionary.* http://www.e-sword.com.

Theophilus of Antioch. *Theophilus to Autolycus,* Book 2, Chapter 15, "Of the Fourth Day." http://www.earlychristianwritings.com/theophilus.html.

Vidal Manzanares, César. *Diccionaro Histórico del Cristianismo* [Historical dictionary of Christianity]. Pamplona, Spain: Verbo Divino, 1999.

Webster's Online Dictionary. All Languages, http://www.websters-online-dictionary.org.

Wickwire, Daniel. *Yahudi, Hıristiyan ve İslâm Kaynaklarına göre Kutsal Kitap'ın Değişmezliği* [The inalterability of the Bible according to Jewish, Christian and Islamic resources]. Istanbul: Lütuf Yayıncılık, 1999.

Wolfson, H. Austryn. *Kelâm Felsefeleri. Müslüman, Hıristiyan ve Yahudi Kelâmı.* Istanbul: Kitapevi Yayınları, 2001. (*Foundations of Religious Philosophy in Judaism, Christianism and Islam.* Cambridge, MA: Harvard University Press, 1974.)

# INDEX OF TERMS

# INDEX OF BIBLICAL REFERENCES

# INDEX OF QUR'ANIC REFERENCES